Your Mind:

The Owner's Manual

by Linda Joy Rose, Ph.D.

BABAJI'S KRIYA YOGA PUBLICATIONS
ST-ETIENNE DE BOLTON, QUEBEC

Your Mind: The Owner's Manual
by Linda Joy Rose, Ph.D

Second International Edition Published in the year 2004

First International Edition Published in September, 1999 by
BABAJI'S KRIYA YOGA AND PUBLICATIONS, INC.
P. O. Box 90, 196 Mountain Road
Eastman, Quebec
Canada, J0E 1P0

Cover design by Michael Tidwell
Graphics by Steven Myhre

Printed and bound in Canada

Canadian Cataloguing in Publication Data
Rose, Linda Joy, 1954-
        Your mind : the owner's manual

        Includes bibliographical references.
        ISBN 1-895383-09-9

        1. Self-actualization (Psychology) I. Title.

BF636.R68 1999   158.1   C99-901136-7

For Ciera Joy – For the privilege of watching you grow up

Acknowledgements

I would like to express my gratitude to the following individuals:

To M. Govindan, my teacher and publisher, for his continued support.

To Karen Sheehan, my friend and publicist. Thank you for always believing in me.

To those dear friends who have guided me with helpful feedback and encouragement – Agnes Guibout, Marilyn Pells Cyr, Drude Clark, Eunice and James Halstead, Dr. Annette LaCasse, Reina Ayala, Dr. Richard Neves, Dr. Nancie Barwick, Connie Warren, and also Michael Tidwell, who graciously designed the cover.

To my father, Werner Rose, for doing his part in getting the word out there.

To my dearest love, Jeff Gerard Horne, mentor and muse.

To all of my teachers and students, past and present, who, through their impact on my life have all contributed to this work.

Thank you.

CONTENTS

Part II: Power Supply (continued)

Part III: Tool Kit   **73**

Part IV: Troubleshooting (continued)

Every day, God gives us the sun –
and also one moment in which we have the ability
to change everything that makes us unhappy.

Everyday, we try to pretend that we haven't perceived that moment,
that it does not exist – that today is the same
as yesterday and will be the same as tomorrow.

But if people really pay attention to their everyday lives,
they will discover that magic moment.
It may arrive in the instant we are doing something mundane...;
It may be hidden in the quiet that follows the lunch hour,
or in the thousand and one things that all seem the same to us.

But that moment exists – a moment when all the power of the stars
becomes a part of us and enables us to perform miracles.

Paulo Coehlo–*By the River Piedra I Sat Down and Wept*

Author's Foreword

Throughout my years of clinical practice many clients expressed frustration and anguish at feeling that they had really botched up their lives. Most of them worried that they were probably repeating the same pattern with their children. An approach that worked best was reminding them that nobody is born with a how-to manual hanging off their big toe! Without specific instructions on how to operate and make full use of this gift of life, we are **all** trying to figure things out—and for most of us it's been hit or miss. This response really seemed to root these clients in the present, and shake them out of obsessing over past mistakes. After all, it does seem logical that if we were never taught the right way to use a priceless piece of machinery, we would likely have to learn by trial and error.

A few years ago my coordinator and sometimes collaborator in Japan, Skip Swanson, was welcoming a new group of interns into my six-month program in alternative mental health therapies. To illustrate his own perspective on how important he considered the information being offered in this course, he pulled out his pocket wizard. (This is a computerized notebook that keeps track of your calendar, appointments, telephone directory, birthdays, things to do, etc.) He told the students that this invaluable tool for organizing his life and increasing his productivity had come with a detailed instruction manual. Without the manual, it would have been hard for him to operate and get the most out of his mini-computer. In his opinion, the adventure that the students were embarking upon was a course on how to realistically operate the mind in order to activate one's full potential.

Considering that the concept of a how-to-manual for the mind seemed to be an on-going theme in my professional life, it became the natural title for this book, and a metaphor for what I have been teaching. The information that I share here was not taught to me as a child. If I had learned the structure and operation of my own mind from an early age I may have avoided a tremendous amount of frustration and futility. I don't regret having had to learn the hard way – this was obviously my path. But I would like to contribute something that helps people have a more hopeful view of life.

In all of the countries or the cultures where I teach, I have discovered a universal yearning for improving one's life experience. However, this seems to go hand in hand with the growing frustration one feels year by year when coming up against a brick wall. Things don't change, yet the yearnings for change don't go away. And this often leads one to the erroneous conclusion that perhaps they are not destined for happiness and success.

People try to change, and fail. This is because they are going after transformation without having the slightest idea of how to make it happen. My goal is to create a book that can realistically show you how to change and make it stick.

Most of the methods that I teach are based on accessing the subconscious mind. This is where you have to go in order to make any change a permanent one, because your subconscious is the seat of your beliefs, your behavior, your emotions, your imagination and your thoughts. This is where you find the raw material that makes you who you are. The best way to reach the subconscious mind is through an *altered state of consciousness*. Any altered state of consciousness is virtually a state of hypnosis.

I once gave a lecture in Guadalajara, Mexico on how hypnosis can be used to alter one's negative childhood programming. After the discussion several people came up to me and chatted privately about how the explanation and diagram had impacted them. A psychologist told me "What you taught here tonight was essentially psychology." "That's right," I replied, "Psychology has a lot of wonderful concepts on how we can improve our lives. But many of these ideas go in one ear and out the other. Through hypnosis we can deliver those concepts to the subconscious mind and put them into action."

A nun came up to me and commented how so much about what I had taught could be related to religious teachings. "Oh yes," I responded, "How can we have mental health without a healthy connection to the divine? Hypnosis can get past the guilt or fear of God that may have been programmed into the subconscious mind. And then we can really feel okay with our Creator." Finally, a young man approached me and said "I've taken a year-long course in metaphysics and feel that what

11

you presented here is inherent in the arcane teachings." "Definitely," I answered, "The esoteric literature contains the Hermetic law that states '*as within, so without*'. If we have chaos in our minds, it will find its expression in our outer world. Hypnosis heals the inside, so that our external reality can reflect the positive transformation."

Each one of these individuals found hypnosis applicable to their arena of expertise. This almost surrealistic occurrence really drove home for me the fact that hypnosis has applications within every area of our lives. This is because the foundation of what makes us who we are is the subconscious mind. Hypnosis is the vehicle that reaches the subconscious and conveys the new ideas and information to be acted upon.

Hypnosis is such a part of our daily lives that it would probably surprise you to know that you go in and out of the hypnotic state at least a dozen times a day and don't even know it. You might think of those times as just daydreaming, or "zoning out", but they are still altered states of consciousness. During these times your subconscious is open and ready to receive your commands.

In this second international edition I want to further explore the concept of "permission levels" — a concept that I briefly touched on in the original text. Permission levels are directly related to the amount of self-esteem and self-love that we have developed. They are internal mechanisms that modulate the amount of enjoyment we permit ourselves to experience, however, they generally operate at a point below consciousness. Giving workshops around the world following the publication of the first edition of this book, I guided participants through original techniques to identify and raise permission levels and most found it to be quite liberating.

I chose for my opening quote a few lines from a book by Paulo Cuehlo, a revered Brazilian writer who has been a tremendous source of inspiration for people all over the world. In this quote he theorizes that God gives us at least one moment every day in which the whole world could open to us if we were to just pay attention and use that moment dynamically. I hope that by the tools and information in this book you will learn to recognize those essential moments and have the confidence to forge ahead.

With these new skills and understanding, may you harness the power of the stars and perform miracles in your life.

Linda Joy Rose, Ph.D.
Newport Beach, California
June 2004

Introduction

Congratulations! You are the owner of the most sophisticated computer that has ever been invented, capable of complex reasoning, deductions, analysis and an unlimited capacity for learning and data storage. It has been estimated that if a model of such a complex machine could be duplicated in physical form – one that could carry out the billions of transactions and messages that cross our minds on a daily basis – it would be the size of the state of Texas! Yet, with such advanced technology gifted to you at birth, you did not come equipped with a how-to manual and it is most likely that you are not benefiting from more than a minute percentage of your computer's capacity. It has also been estimated that we use perhaps only between 3-5% of our mind's potential. That is like spending your hard-earned money on a cutting edge computer and never learning how to properly operate it to get the maximum benefit for your investment.

In addition to the manifold operations of the mind in processing and storing information and enabling us to learn consistently, the mind is also the key factor in the creation of our personal reality. In other words, our thought processes manifest our physical experiences. (As the biblical saying "*as a man thinketh in his heart, so shall he live*") Although we tend to assume that thoughts are random and entirely subjective, they represent the true nature of our subconscious content. We go through the day virtually oblivious of the effect that repetitive and unexamined thoughts have on our existence. And then year by year we tend to get a little more frustrated, a little more depressed and finally convinced that somehow true happiness or success have left us by the wayside. Yet, imagine discovering that by implementing the easy-to-learn rules and suggestions in this manual, you could enhance your life experience a hundred-fold!

So much of whom you assume yourself to be is the result of the programming you received during the first twelve years of your life. The way you see yourself, life and the world in general has been formed by the impressions you received during those crucial years of development. When you buy a new computer for your home or office you usually have some software programs automatically installed which you have the option to change or upgrade. If the accompanying programs are not compatible to your needs you would simply replace them with the proper ones. When was the last time you searched your own data base to find out if the programming that "automatically" came with your mind is one that serves you for your higher needs and goals? Would you even know how to run a search on that data base? And if you did, would you know how to alter the programming so that it worked according to your specifications? Herein lies the purpose of this manual, a how-to guide on how to bring forth the full potential from the most extraordinary gift that you have ever received.

It is my purpose, in sharing this instruction manual with you, that you become conscious of what your mind is telling you about yourself and giving you the option to reject or override those thoughts or suggestions that are not getting you what you want in life. All action comes about by orders from your mind. Your behavior is the result of suggestions that have been implanted in your mind either consciously or unconsciously. A suggestion is a word, series of words or phrases that once recorded upon the subconscious mind will bring about a certain behavior, result or condition. These suggestions are the result of programming. Anything that you have accomplished up to this point in your life is the result of a suggestion or series of suggestions currently present in your subconscious mind. Conversely, anything that you have not been able to accomplish up to now in your life is the result of a suggestion or series of suggestions currently present in your subconscious mind. In order to change your life experience you need to change the programming.

If your computer had a glitch that made it respond in an erroneous way or not carry out a specific command, you would need to get to the source of the problem in order to repair it. Unless you were an expert in software design it is unlikely that you would be able to fix the problem without knowing how to communicate to the computer in its particular language. You would have to possess technical information in order to give the command to correct the problem. The subconscious also operates by means of commands given to it in a set language. It can only respond to what is presented in a certain vernacular, just as computers are programmed in technical languages. Although the rules and laws of the mind are relatively simple to learn, there is the element of having to study and learn these techniques in order to bring about positive change. It would be foolish and potentially dangerous to operate a sophisticated piece of equipment without first studying its proper usage. If you were the experimental type, you might have some successes, but they would be hit or miss. Once you realize how the mind works, you have a whole panorama of possibilities laid out before you.

This text is divided into four sections, each with a certain goal:

Section One, entitled *Operation and Structure*, will teach you how the mind is divided into conscious and subconscious and what jurisdiction each part has over your life. You will learn about how we are programmed and what effect programming has over our attitudes, thoughts, feelings and actions. The laws of the mind outlined in this section should give a clear understanding of how our personal reality is created via our thoughts as well as clarifying the concept that we are truly capable of changing our life experience through the power of suggestion.

Section Two, entitled *Power Supply*, will take you into the realm of thought, energy, and suggestion – the fuel sources that run the mind. You will be introduced to the concept of the Human Energy Field and discover how certain thoughts get trapped into that space and reflect negative perceptions back to our minds. You will learn about the phenomena that exist as potentials within our subconscious mind and how to develop them consciously and through altered states. You will discover the concepts of *intentional* and *unintentional states of hypnosis* and how often we are responsive to suggestions and programming without even being aware of these states.

Section Three is your *Tool Kit*. Here you are given specific instructions and techniques to enhance the functioning of your mind and improve the quality of your life. You will learn the *21-Day Secret*, a realistic and amazing tool to bring about life-affirming behavioral changes in as little as three weeks. Easy-to-implement methods for relaxing your mind and body and entering altered states at will are outlined in this section, and you will also learn how to supercharge your goals and desires through the skills of imagery and visualization.

In the final section, *Troubleshooting*, we will go deeper into the area of programming to clear the source of some of those negative emotions and attitudes that may have been holding you back from being fully present within your physical reality. While you might want to consider working directly with a hypnotherapist or psychologist if you have had major traumas or severe issues, there is much that you can do on your own to clear these limiting patterns from your subconscious as well as your energy field. The technique entitled "Reprogramming the Data Base" is the first stage in clearing the old programs and patterns that no longer serve you as a mature, evolving adult. Subsequent techniques will assist you in comprehending how certain statements that you were told may have inadvertently set you on a path contrary to what you may presently desire. In this section you will also study the connection between mind and body and ascertain where certain beliefs and negative suggestions may be influencing your health and/or body image.

I have designed this guide to be simplistic even though we are dealing with concepts that are complex and at times, mind-boggling. This truly is just an introduction to the marvels of your mind. Once you begin to understand clearly how your mind works and take the responsibility to implement some techniques to alter your life experience I believe that a whole new world of opportunity will open to you. You will begin to see yourself as co-creator with the Divine and look forward to the myriad possibilities that await you each and every day that you sojourn on this earth.

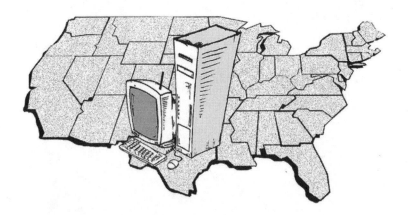

A computer that could carry out your mind's billions of daily
transactions would be the size of Texas!

Part I: Operation and Structure

We are what we think.
All that we are arises with our thoughts.
With our thoughts we make the world.

The Buddha

The Tip of the Iceberg

By now just about everyone on the planet has seen the movie *Titanic*. Even if you haven't sat through the entire film, it's likely that you have seen some of the previews—particularly the scene where two men in the lookout perch are trying to keep themselves warm in the freezing Atlantic air. Suddenly, they see a huge mountain of ice looming dead ahead and shout into the phone "Iceberg – straight ahead!"

That immense mountain of ice comprises only about 10% of the iceberg's mass, with the other 90% below the surface of the water. This is an ideal metaphor for the **conscious** and **subconscious minds.**

As massive and impressive as our consciousness seems to us, with its ability to reason, think logically, solve complex puzzles and send shuttles into space, it represents only approximately 12% of our total mind power. That means that the most powerful part of our mind is below the surface of consciousness – *the subconscious comprises about 88% of the mind's capacity*! It wasn't the chunks of ice falling onto the deck as the ship grazed the iceberg that sunk the *Titanic*. What caused the fatalities that night was the damage done below deck, beneath the surface of the water. Where we most fail in *our* efforts to change our life experience is expecting that paltry 12% of consciousness to overpower the enormity of our subconscious minds.

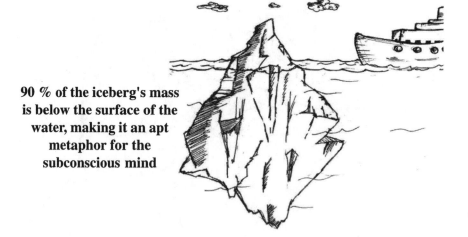

90 % of the iceberg's mass is below the surface of the water, making it an apt metaphor for the subconscious mind

The Deeper Levels of Mind

Before birth and in the early years of our lives the subconscious mind is more active. Within the subconscious is the autonomic nervous system (ANS), which controls all of the involuntary processes of the body, such as circulation, respiration, digestion and elimination. The autonomic nervous system also controls the flight or fight response, which is a self-preservation reaction that we inherited from our cave dweller ancestors

When primitive man faced a threat to his well being, he had one of two options: stay and fight – or run away. Imminent danger sent a signal automatically from the brain stem, via a nerve along one side of the spinal column – the sympathetic nerve. This enervated the smooth muscles of the body, such as the heart, and stimulated the pumping of blood to the extremities via the release of the hormone adrenaline. With increased strength in his arms and legs, primitive man could then battle his enemy or rapidly escape.

Once the danger had passed, the parasympathetic nerve, running along the other side of the spine, would send a signal to release a calming endorphin hormone in order to return the body to the state of homeostasis. This is the state where our body functions optimally and for most of the time. Our modern day ANS functions in the same way. Any stress factor activates the flight and fight syndrome, launching our bodies into a state of agitation. Subsequently the parasympathetic nerve releases the hormones to bring us back to the status quo. Due to the incredible stimuli of daily life, our modern ANS is constantly mobilized, which lowers our immune response and exposes us to disease.

This deeper level of the subconscious is called the primitive mind, (see diagram of The Structure of the Mind on page 24) because it comes genetically pre-programmed with certain instincts, impulses and inherited fears. The primitive mind comprises roughly 10% of the total mind power. An instinct is something that we have an innate knowledge of, such as a baby who begins to suck the moment the nipple is introduced. An impulse is something that we do reflexively, such as ducking if an object comes flying at our heads. Certain kinds of fears are inborn such as falling and loud noises. Throughout our childhood we also discover what is threatening to our well being, and those learned fears will also automatically activate the flight or fight response. Even situations that resemble or are associated to those learned fears will instantly stimulate the stress response and exhaust our resources. How many times have we heard that we must *"try to control stress"*, or *"just relax and you'll be fine"*? Attempting to relax oneself through an act of will is futile unless you can get to the core of the fear and deactivate the autogenic response.

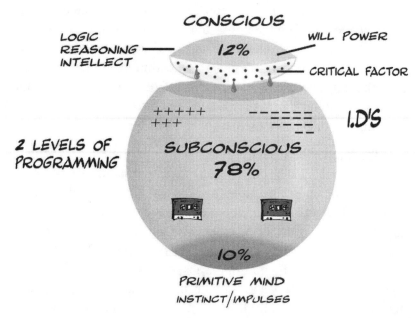

The Structure of the Mind

Identifications

One level up and still part of the subconscious is what we call the *modern mind*. This is where we receive the programming that differentiates us as individuals. While this will continue developing throughout our lifetime, it is most active between the ages of zero to 13. We begin receiving impulses even in the neo-natal state, which has been substantiated by many researchers. Working with clients using hypnotic age regression, I found that a high percentage of traumatic experience involves the pre-natal perceptions. Negative self-image and self-defeating behaviors can be traced back to the womb where some of these individuals perceived that they were not really wanted or that the circumstances surrounding their births were not favorable.

The most important characteristic of the subconscious mind is the *programming*. This is where we receive the input that results in our development of a unique personality. There are two levels of programming.

The first level is what we acquire directly from those persons most influential during our upbringing: parents, grandparents, siblings, caretakers, teachers, etc. We obtain from them a certain world-view, colored by the society we were raised in, our cultural beliefs, religious creeds, taboos, prejudices and traditions. As if we had a series of tiny cassette tapes in this part of the mind, we are literally recording the overall belief systems of our predecessors. Have you ever said something automatically and then exclaimed "My goodness, I just sounded exactly like my mother!"? This illustrates how a portion of our programming is channeled directly into our subconscious minds.

The next avenue of programming is very significant as it forms the foundation of our belief systems about ourselves, life, and the world, in general. Through exposure to life experience, traces are formed upon the subconscious that we call identifications. This is a subjective interpretation of the experience—a value judgment that is strictly up to the perception of the individual. Identifications can be positive, negative, or neutral. Virtually all of our behavioral patterns are generated from the unconscious naming of experiences. According to Roberto Assagioli, founder of Psychosynthesis, one of the main functions of the unconscious is the assimilation of what has been perceived and learned. The internal elaboration of experience is one of the most important stages in the educational process.[1]

For example, two male siblings, nine and eight years of age, witness a serious car accident. One of the boys becomes very involved in the activity, getting close to the paramedics, trying to be helpful where he can. The other brother has nearly fainted on the spot. The first boy has identified the experience in a positive manner. The identification is recorded onto the mind in the form of a certain thought or idea. In this case let's say that the identification is that this young man is capable of facing adversity in a composed manner. This now becomes the basis of a belief system that will subsequently generate attitudes, feelings, thoughts, habits and actions, paving the way for future behavioral patterns. Maybe some day he will become a doctor, or maybe he's just the kind of person you always want to have around in case of an emergency.

The second brother, while having the same experience, has "told" his mind something quite different. It could be something to the effect that "life is quite uncertain". This will form a world-view unlike that of his brother's resulting in an entirely different set of behavioral patterns. Although the origin of the pattern will remain unconscious to him, some of his attitudes and conducts throughout his lifetime will have been generated from that experience.

Repetitive experience also leaves its trace upon the subconscious mind. For instance, if we are told constantly that we are unworthy, or unattractive, or at fault, identifications will be formed accordingly. So much of whom we believe ourselves to be is based upon erroneous conclusions that we have drawn due to our subjective interpretations of experience. In the *Troubleshooting* section of the book I will suggest several techniques and exercises to get to the core of some of these patterns and show you how to neutralize the hold they have over your behavior.

Beliefs Hold the Key

At the root of every identification exists a belief. This is a statement of relative truth that generates a series of attitudes, feelings, thoughts and behaviors. Once programming has been set, the subconscious mind holds on to the pattern. By the time we are twelve years of age, a filter forms over the subconscious for the purpose of protecting our programming. This is called the critical factor of the mind. So whether our programming was good, bad, right, wrong, beneficial or detrimental, it is locked in the recesses of our minds and is generally inaccessible to our conscious awareness. In other words, you can believe something or act a certain way and not have a clue as to why. The programming compels your behavior and will continue to do so until the subconscious is told otherwise.

The beliefs that we carry will ultimately be recreated in our life experience. They are the building blocks to our physical reality, just as DNA strands are the building blocks to our physical bodies.

My husband and I were on a trip to Bali once. We had such a good experience at a certain restaurant that we decided to go back again for dinner a few nights later. The hostess remembered us and spent some time chatting at our table. This lovely young woman shared her ambitions about getting a better job and becoming successful, but a few moments later added that it was unlikely that she would ever get ahead. When I probed to find out why she had such a hopeless outlook on life she replied that "in this world the rich get richer and the poor get poorer". "Is that how you really want things to be?" I asked her. "Do you really believe you live in a world where you can never get ahead because you were born at the wrong end of society?" By challenging her she began to understand that she had been programmed with a belief system that would ultimately prevent her from getting ahead. Her family members had simply passed on what they had been taught without ever considering that this was a limiting idea.

It doesn't do any good to blame our limitations on faulty programming or misinformation supplied by our parents or caretakers. They did the best that they could do with what they had been taught. They were only operating on automatic pilot, adding a new link to the endless chain of ignorance and limitation passed on from generation to generation. Blaming will not change the programming, nor will it take you one inch closer to getting what you want in life. By taking the responsibility to analyze what was channeled into your subconscious as a child, either deliberately or inadvertently, you will gain an enormous amount of self-knowledge. Then you have the option of changing the messages that no longer serve you for your highest good.

To summarize:

- *Programming is the subconscious input.*
- *Identifications are etched into the subconscious.*
- *Identifications are subjective interpretations of experience.*
- *At the core of every identification exists a belief.*
- *Beliefs generate attitudes.*
- *Attitudes generate feelings.*
- *Feelings generate thoughts.*
- *Thoughts generate action.*
- *What we experience in life is generally related to the core belief system.*

Other Characteristics of the Subconscious

The subconscious is the seat of our emotions and our imagination. For this reason it is the part of the mind associated with feelings. Every experience that you have ever been exposed to through your five senses is recorded upon the subconscious mind, however, very little of that information makes its way to conscious awareness. This data is stored away into file cabinets and is retrieved and acted upon when needed.

This part of our mind has a very child-like aspect. It accepts uncritically what it has been told and comes to decisions based on that information. Suggestions tend to be embraced indiscriminately providing they do not pose any moral or physical threat. For this reason, this part of the mind is sometimes referred to as a servo-mechanism. Once given a task it will relentlessly proceed towards realization of that goal. It is the dynamo that directs our energy.[2]

The subconscious operates by way of inductive reasoning rather than deductive – moving from the particular to the general. For example, a mother constantly tells her child that only naughty little boys and girls get sick. Then, should the child contract an illness such as the chicken pox, the conclusion that results in the mind of the child is "I am bad." This is where we tend to get into a lot of trouble – the subconscious is entirely sentimental and irrational. Logic is not a characteristic of the unconscious. For that reason, the unfortunate identification "I am bad" continues to govern behavior as long as it goes unchallenged.

26

The subconscious is a servo-mechanism designed to produce according to your conscious direction.

The Critical Factor

The protective filter separating the subconscious from the conscious mind is called the critical factor. It is a narrow band that serves as the dividing line and also acts as a filter between the two levels of mind. In the illustration of the iceberg, it can be likened to the water line. The critical factor keeps our programming intact and also protects the conscious mind from becoming overwhelmed by the billions of message units coming in each day. And because the subconscious is so vulnerable to suggestion, it keeps it from acting upon every order it is given.

Children are exceptionally susceptible to suggestion because the critical factor does not really start forming until about six years of age. It is fully operative by the time we are twelve and our programming is pretty much complete. With the subconscious mind virtually wide open for the first six years of life, it is understandable how damaged we can become through negative programming. John Bradshaw theorized that children spend the first six years of their lives in a hypnotic trance, which is essentially the subconscious-dominant state.[3]

The critical factor acts as a watchman, guarding the gateway to the subconscious, so that nothing will enter that does not conform to one's original programming. This is what usually keeps us from making a significant change or being able to overcome the effect of our childhood programming. It only allows data to penetrate the subconscious that corresponds with the identifications and belief systems that are in place.

Greg, for example, is shy and believes himself to be very unpopular. This insecurity stems from an experience in childhood when a group of kids from his school ridiculed him. I invite him to stand up before an audience of 50. Each member of the audience tells him what a great and worthy person he has become. This is probably very motivating to Greg and for a few hours he is filled with self-confidence. But, by the next morning he is once again plagued by doubts about his self-worth. The critical factor—not finding any belief system to support his newfound confidence—effectively repelled the data and barred it from accessing the subconscious. If the group had booed and embarrassed him, the critical factor would have evaluated that input to be congruent with the former programming. In that case, the original identification would become even more deeply ingrained, and Greg would continue to feel victimized by his insecurity.

The subconscious is only freely accessed when the critical factor "steps aside". This happens naturally when it becomes overwhelmed by serious illness, shock, extreme anxiety, intense emotions, and natural disasters. All of these can be classified as *unintentional states of hypnosis*. The critical factor may also be gently shifted by techniques involving inner focus and progressive relaxation, allowing free passage into the unconscious realms.

The Conscious Mind

Our conscious mind provides awareness. It receives information through the sense organs and connects us to the outer world. Through the conscious faculty we make intellectual decisions, analyze, and form conclusions by way of both inductive and deductive reasoning. The conscious mind is the facility used to gather and analyze information for storage in the brain's memory bank, while the subconscious uses that stored information to operate the body processes. Before any data is allowed to be stored for further use, the conscious mind first considers the validity of the information. If the data cannot be classified as believable, important or true, it gets rejected.[4]   Most suggestions presented to the conscious mind are automatically discarded as false statements.

Other vital functions of the conscious mind include sorter-of-information, decision-maker, and judge. Will power—our capacity to act upon our desires—generates from the conscious mind, as well. This aspect of the mind is ruled by logic, absorbing information through the five senses and reasoning through the inductive and deductive processes.

Desires vs. Beliefs

I would probably be hard-pressed to find someone who did not desire more success, happiness and abundance in their life. Ambition, striving for excellence, and yearning to improve our life experience are all fairly universal human traits no matter where you go in the world; as a result, there does not seem to be any lack of desire for change.

With all of these noble intentions, why then do we fall short of realizing our desires? Why does the average New Year's resolution fizzle out before the third week in January? Take a look at that iceberg again. The part of the mind that generates desires represents only roughly 10% of its potency. Beliefs reside in the part that is nine times stronger! Whenever there is a battle between desire and belief, belief prevails. In a struggle between willpower and imagination, imagination is the victor. When logic goes to war with sentimentality, sentimentality is going to win out. It's just a numbers game. If I were to hand you one end of a rope that passed through a hole in the wall, giving the other end of the rope to nine people of your approximate height and build, it doesn't matter how strong and determined you were. Eventually you would tire and give up. The other side would win by sheer force.

There's nothing wrong with having the desire to change; in fact, it's wonderful to want to improve yourself. But, unless your belief systems are congruent with your intention, you've set yourself up for a losing battle.

Carlos was a foreman in a factory making a good living and enjoying many benefits such as health care and pension plan. He became interested in real estate and took all of the necessary courses to obtain his license. In the beginning he was only able to devote his weekends to this new career, but it became apparent that without a full commitment, he would never be able to fully move forward in his field. He wanted to take that leap of faith, but the idea of giving up the security of his day job terrified him. It seemed that the more he tried to talk himself out of his fear, the more paralyzed he became.

As we probed into his subconscious beliefs, he recalled his father continually criticizing him as a child. Time and time again he was told that he couldn't do anything right. This led to an *identification* that he was not worthy. Carlos' desire to devote himself to a job that provided the opportunity to feed his passion was insignificant compared to the fear he had of failing and living out his negative judgments. By understanding and applying the laws of the mind, Carlos neutralized his limiting belief and was able to muster the confidence needed to take the risk. I heard a few months later that he had been top salesman in his office for two months in a row!

The Laws of the Mind

At the turn of the century there was a lot of interest in the study of hypnosis. The Mecca for those students fascinated by the relatively new discipline was France, home to some of the most important schools of hypnosis. One school theorized that the trance state was sufficient for healing while another advocated the use of suggestion combined with hypnosis. But a French pharmacist by the name of Emile Coué formulated certain laws of the mind that supported his theory of auto-suggestion. According to Coué, no trance state is needed in order to program the subconscious: simple self-suggestion is sufficient, provided the suggestions are designed along certain laws and used repetitively. It was Coué who coined the phrase, "Every day, in every way, I'm getting better and better and better."

Coué's first law is the **Law of Concentrated Attention**. This law states that whenever your attention is focused on an idea, that idea tends to realize itself. Specifically, it defines how you learned any skill or talent that you may have acquired, and determines how all habits, good or bad are formed. The *Law of Concentrated Attention* is the basis of the *21-Day Secret*. The subconscious is a servo-mechanism, designed to produce according to your conscious direction. You may want to conceive of it as a genie in a lamp; similarly, concentrating your attention on an idea consistently and repetitively is like rubbing the lamp so that you can get your wish.

When you concentrate your attention on any idea or thought form, it becomes reality to you. For instance, if on a daily basis you are prone to saying that you "just can't get anywhere in life", there is an enormous amount of energy being directed to that notion. As if a laser were being beamed on this thought, it becomes a focal point. This is how negative statements become self-fulfilling prophecies. No wonder getting ahead feels like swimming upstream! Your *desire* to get ahead is totally voided by the amount of *concentrated energy* focused on a negative thought form.

Concentrating your attention on an idea consistently and repetitively is like rubbing the lamp so that you can get your wish

It has been estimated that approximately 70% of our daily self-talk is negative![5] Instead of concentrating our energy on our strengths, we tend to focus on what seems to be lacking in ourselves and in our lives. This only magnifies the intensity of the laser beam. You are literally directing your genie to perpetuate a state of deficiency. This is why it is so important to be aware of our thoughts, especially when the subconscious becomes dominant. This is the state of *unintentional hypnosis* (which you will learn about in the next section) in which you are particularly receptive to suggestion. By continuing to express yourself in an unfavorable way, you are only emphasizing the core of the belief system.

Once you learn how to deliver suggestions in the language of the subconscious this law of the mind is a blessing. Where it might have been working against you because of your lack of awareness, the *Law of Concentrated Attention* becomes your key to manifesting a much more joyful and successful existence.

Coué's second law is the **Law of Reversed Effect**. This law states that the harder you try to do something, the less you are able to do it. For instance, if I were to invite you to close your eyes and think about any pleasant object that you may choose, but under no circumstances should you visualize a pink elephant, your mental screen would have a whole stampede of them marching across it!

Whenever we get the clue that we need to change a behavior in order to get ahead, we usually frame it in our minds as "I'm going to try to do this differently". Whether it is organizing your paper work, communicating better with your spouse, saving money, or losing weight, the moment you verbally or mentally state "I'll try", you cancel the order to your servo-mechanism. Try is simply not perceived as a valid request by your genie!

Think about times that you tried to fall asleep—the more you tried, the more sleep seemed to elude you. Another element of the Law of

Reversed Effect is that the problem becomes more pronounced when emotion is tied in with the attempt. This unfortunately is the basis of certain sexual dysfunction, such as premature ejaculation: the more a man tries to retain his orgasm, the less he is able to do so.

Since a belief system is already locked in place—telling the subconscious that something is not attainable or viable—the act of trying is not able to override programming. Let's say that a woman carries a belief system that she is unworthy of love. She is not likely to be consciously aware of this belief, yet she desperately wants to be loved. She will then attract a series of relationships that "prove" her unworthiness. Or perhaps, she cannot seem to find anyone to love her. The more she tries, the more futile each attempt becomes. A good metaphor would be like chasing a feather—your momentum would keep pushing it beyond your reach. The only way for this woman to experience her heart's desire is to get to the core issue, that she does not believe herself to be worthy of love. Once that is released and reprogrammed, she can then create different experiences for herself.

This is why it is imperative for you to eliminate the word *try* from any form of self-suggestion or any of the tools in your kit. *Try* automatically activates the *Law of Reversed Effect* and cancels out your most positive intentions.

Whenever you are sure that you are unable to do something, attempting to override it by sheer willpower is wasted energy. First you need to change the programming; otherwise, it's fruitless to go to battle with the part of your mind that's nine times stronger! Use the tools provided in this book to change the negative belief that you "cannot" do something, then your thoughts and actions will follow the new belief.

Coué's third law is the **Law of Dominant Effect**. This law states that the suggestion presented to the mind carrying the most powerful emotion will displace any other suggestion in the mind at the time. For instance, imagine a trip to the beach to enjoy a celebration with a group of your friends, a day filled with laughter, music, sharing and play. Suddenly you are drawn to a commotion at the edge of the water where a young child has drowned --the feelings of joy would be replaced immediately by feelings of shock and sorrow. Those emotions dominate as they are more powerful.

Feelings of guilt often overpower the desire for success. Low self-esteem tends to win out over a longing for approval. Unfortunately, the stronger emotions are usually the ones that are the most damaging.

In terms of your striving to get ahead, this means that is if you have deep-seated feelings of self-rejection, these are likely to carry more energy than your conscious goals. I have known many brilliant and talented individuals, whom in spite of having come up with sure-fire ideas for success, invariably failed due to an opposing belief system in the subconscious. If your programming says you are a failure, you will somehow sabotage your most valiant efforts to get ahead.

To illustrate this law, I use the following analogy in my classes. Picture a metal table covered with metal shavings. Underneath the table you are holding a magnet. Wherever you drag the magnet, the shavings are drawn. The *Law of Dominant Effect* means that the energy of the mind is magnetized by the governing emotion. This explains why it is not sufficient to simply wish for something to be in order to bring it into manifestation. If you desire abundance but carry a belief system that *"it is easier for the camel to go through the eye of the needle than the rich man to enter the kingdom of heaven"*, then the dominant effect will be the fear that having money will be your ultimate downfall. As the magnet is drawn towards the fear, the opposite effect of the desire will be realized.

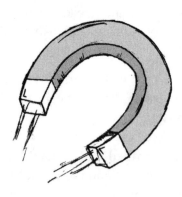

At any given moment there is only a certain amount of energy available in the brain which invariably is channeled to the strongest emotional wish or feeling in the present.[6] This makes the point that our emotions influence our state of mind. The subconscious mind is ruled by imagination, the conscious mind is ruled by willpower. In any conflict between imagination and willpower, the imagination is bound to win. But the good news is, **imagination can be directed!**[7] I have provided a valuable *Tool Kit* with in-depth instructions, in order to teach you how to direct your imagination.

Part II: Power Supply

Ideas float all around you but so often
you won't see!
When you seek inspiration, it's ideas you want.
When you pray for guidance, it's ideas
that show the way.
But you have to pay attention!
And it's up to you to put ideas to work.

Richard Bach

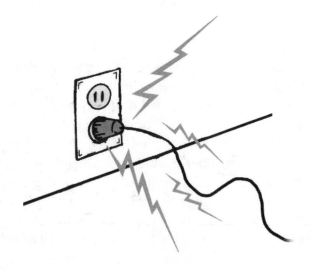

The Creative Power of Thought

In the old paradigm of science, know as Newtonian physics, it was believed that although *energy* and *matter* co-exist within this universe, the two are mutually exclusive. In other words, matter cannot influence energy, nor does energy have any effect on matter. The new paradigm, called quantum physics, has developed a very different perspective. Through experimentation the modern view is that matter and energy are, in essence, equal. Everything in the universe is composed of energy— tiny particles vibrating at varying speeds. Matter is just a more condensed form of energy, that vibrates at a rather slow pace. At the other end of the spectrum are thoughts, which are more fluid and mobile and vibrate at the speed of light.[8]

The idea that thoughts, feelings, or emotions could have any impact on one's physical body was anathema to the majority of mainstream medical practitioners, based on the Newtonian school of thought. Since the body is matter, how could thoughts – a mere energy – have any influence? It was not until very recently that the role of the subconscious mind has been acknowledged in the development of illness. This has lead to a fairly new discipline within the medical field *(psychoneuroimmunology)* that studies the effect of mind over body, acknowledging that energy and matter are interdependent.

First year medical students studied the *placebo effect* for many decades, yet were still reluctant to give any credence to the idea that thought could have any power over our physical functions. The placebo effect is what occurs when an experimental drug is given to two different groups to test the outcome. One of the groups is given the actual medicine while the other is given a pill that is filled with inert ingredients. Both groups are told what the medicine is expected to accomplish. When tested at a later time, many subjects in the "sugar pill" group show the same improvements as those taking the actual drug. This is strong evidence that the mind can play a crucial role in the healing process, however, since it did not fit in with the accepted model of science, the placebo effect was generally brushed aside and not given much credence.

Just as our thoughts have the ability to tap into our physical bodies, they also have a continuous effect on our physical realities. According to Shakti Gawain thought manifests instantaneously. "Thoughts and feelings have their own magnetic energy, which attracts energy of a similar nature"[9]

We tend to consider our thoughts as arising haphazardly, not at all connected to our physical reality—mere "things" that belong only to our subjective worlds and of no particular consequence. Yet, a person's thoughts are seldom random, disjointed entities.[10] Every thought that we have vibrates into the outer world and attracts a concrete manifestation of its feeling tone. Positive thoughts go out into the world and produce a positive experience. Negative thoughts travel outwards and reply negatively. More simply put, *"as you sow, so shall you reap"*.

Therefore, the primary power supply of your mind is thought. Thoughts are generally reflections of the ideas that your belief systems hold, as well as the collective beliefs of the community that surrounds you. Thoughts are the natural offspring of the identifications that were programmed in your subconscious during the first years of life. Without delving into the origin of these thought forms and questioning the validity of the belief systems, or consciously evaluating your thoughts, you are at the mercy of your creations in the outer world.

The First Thought

The power behind your thought comes from the identification. This is what you learned to believe about yourself, life, or the world in general in your early years. For example, if you constantly question yourself about the trustworthiness of the people in your life, you might have identified that the "world is an unsafe place." I call this core idea the *first thought*.

Neale Donald Walsch, in *Conversations with God"*, refers to this as the Sponsoring Thought. "It is either a thought of love or fear. It is the thought behind the thought *behind* the thought. It is the first thought. It is prime force. It is the raw energy that drives the engine of human experience."[11]

A student in one of my classes asked me, "I often think about getting a new job, one in which I will be appreciated for my good work and paid a decent wage. If my thoughts are constantly creating my reality, why aren't those thoughts attracting a better job for me?" The answer would be to examine the first thought. As you learned in Part I, desire is not enough to make a change. If the belief is stronger than the desire, it will ultimately win out. If the first thought has to do with a sense of unworthiness, thoughts of a new job can't generate enough energy to magnetize that experience. The underlying thought is what radiates out and perpetuates reality.

In my mid-thirties I had a busy hypnotherapy practice in the Hispanic community in Los Angeles. With the development of a line of programming tapes in Spanish I was hoping to establish my financial independence even though I had a very affluent lifestyle supported by my husband's profession. However, a first thought was holding me back from achieving my independence. An affirmation that I used often was "I am successful, abundant and financially independent". Every time that I made this statement, I could feel a slight wrenching sensation in the center of my chest. It was as if I didn't really believe what I was saying.

This went on for about six months until one day I decided to challenge myself. I spoke out loud with conviction about my desire to make it on my own, yet my inner voice was contradicting that statement. There was obviously something in my programming that did not agree with my desire to break away from the comfort of being fully supported. Finally, I chose to enter the trance state and use a technique I'd developed (see *Troubleshooting* for "Discovering the First Thought"); as a result, I had a very clear image of myself as a child being told by my father that I would always have a man to take care of me. I could see him telling me that "it was okay to be cute and smart, but I'd always have the financial support of my daddy or a husband". So, naturally the thought behind the thought that made my heart clench every time I declared my future independence, was that as a woman I could not make it without a man's support. No matter how much I desired to be free of that, it was not going to change until I changed my belief system. So, I created a script (see *Tool Kit* for "Rules of

Suggestion") and modified that belief system to one that supported my future vision and goals. Although my husband and I have parted ways, we remain very good friends. I went out successfully on my own and am satisfied to report that my ex-husband has sought me out many times in the past few years for short-term loans!

The Problem with Prayer

Many times it appears that our prayers are being ignored. A contributing factor is that we are ignoring the first thought. You can urgently pray for help to get out of a difficult situation, but at the same time carry a belief system that you are guilty and deserve to be punished. Your desire to be rescued is canceled out by the negative belief that you are getting your just desserts. You have to believe in the positive outcome in order for a prayer to be answered.

There is a scripture in the Bible that lays this out very simply and clearly. *"Listen to Me. You can pray for anything, and if you believe you will have it."* Mark 11:24. This would tend to place the responsibility on **you** to investigate the sources of your belief systems by probing the subconscious mind. Without congruency between your petition and the underlying belief it is unlikely that your prayers will be answered in the way that you'd expect.

The Power of Suggestion

The subconscious mind has its own language. It is called *suggestion*. Suggestion is a word, group of words, images, phrases, ideas or concepts that instructs the subconscious to reorganize its thoughts or actions. We are continuously exposed to suggestions, either by way of our own thought processes, the media, persons in positions of authority and prestige, or those individuals who impact our lives. A suggestion conveys the idea to our subconscious to be acted upon. The placebo effect, which was discussed earlier in this chapter, illustrated how the implied suggestion that the pill was going to improve a certain condition, activated the subconscious to carry this out.

Dr. Larry Dossey, a visionary physician who has written much about the power of prayer in the healing process, has also seen the opposite of the placebo effect generated through negative beliefs and suggestions. This can lead to what he calls a "self-hex". In his book, *Be Careful What You Pray For...* he writes: "We physicians often deny the reality of hexes spells and curses, but we have a version of the same thing: the *nocebo* effect. The nocebo and placebo effects are opposites. The latter refers to the *positive* physical effects that occur as a result of belief, expectation, and suggestion. In contrast, nocebo effects are the *negative* results of negative beliefs, feelings and emotions. Nocebo effects are essentially self-curses."[12]

During my years of practice in the Hispanic community I was astounded at how many of my clients believed that bad luck or failed relationships were caused by hexes placed on them by an enemy or rival. The practice of *brujeria* (witchcraft) is prevalent in many cultures throughout the world. I clearly recognized that the greatest harm was coming from the power of suggestion, not from the *brujo* (witch doctor). The belief that they could be ruined by a hex was the primary force in manifesting their unfortunate experiences. Once the negative suggestions were counteracted by positive ones, these clients overcame the idea that they had been victimized.

Suggestions, thoughts, intentions, words, and beliefs, whether they are conscious or unconscious, set energy in motion and on a path to creation. Gary Zukav, author of the thought-provoking bestseller, *Seat of the Soul*, cautions that "your intentions create the reality that you experience. Until you become aware of this, it happens unconsciously. Therefore, be mindful of what you project. That is the first step toward authentic power."[13] Ultimately, what we think is what we live.

The Mind Field

Our thoughts seem to swim within the space between our ears, but new research points to the fact that thoughts actually occupy the electromagnetic field that surrounds our body. Since the advent of quantum medicine and the recognition that we are energy beings, scientists have conceded that we possess a higher vibratory body that extends out several inches beyond our physical boundaries. This is called the Human Energy Field (HEF) and has been measured by sophisticated equipment and Kirlian photography, but is still in the early stages of investigation. Richard Gerber, author of *Vibrational Medicine,* suggests that these higher energy bodies are unseen because the technologies to make them visible to the human eye are still in the developmental stages. This etheric body (as he calls the HEF) interacts with the physical system through "specific channels of energy exchange which allow the flow of energetic information to move from one system to another."[14]

Valerie Hunt, a professor of kinesiology at UCLA believes that the mind is not physically located in the brain, but rather in the electromagnetic field.[15] This is supported by Caroline Myss, who writes that this Field "contains and reflects each individual's energy...created by our internal and external experiences – both positive and negative."[16]

In esoteric philosophy the Human Energy Field is called the aura. Although I refer to it as the Mind Field, other names that I have heard include the Quantum Body, the Morphic Field, the Outer Mind or Extra-Conscious. The Mind Field works as a kind of antenna or radar that picks up data and signals from the outside world and transmits it back to our conscious minds for analysis and decision-making. Although we have the illusion of separateness, it is the Mind Field that connects us to every other being on the planet through what is called the Unified Field. Experiments with group meditation by practitioners of Transcendental Meditation (also know as TM) for war-torn cities, such as Beirut, Lebanon or violence-ridden inner cities have demonstrated that the collective group consciousness was able to affect an increase in harmony and a decrease in stress and violence.

The Mind Field also works like a two-way mirror in that it reflects the images, feelings, perceptions, and inner voices generated from the belief systems of our subconscious mind. Thus, we become virtually surrounded by trapped fears and judgments that were erroneously implanted due to faulty programming in our youth. Our world-view and self-view become extremely distorted as we are bombarded by the negative feelings, images and voices of our past. These stimuli additionally cause us to react to what we have become conditioned to, consider threats to our survival and ultimately activate the fight or flight response.

For instance, if your Field contains a memory of your father's fre-

43

quent bouts of rage, just seeing your boss getting mildly upset could trigger a stress reaction. You might be over-reacting, but your perception of personal experience is colored by the thought forms trapped in the Field. Even by just imagining that your boss is mad at you, the same perception of an imminent threat would be reflected back to your primitive mind and start the production of adrenaline and other stimulants in your system. Deepak Chopra concurs in *The 7 Spiritual Laws of Success*: "Most of us, as a result of conditioning, have repetitious and predictable responses to the stimuli in our environment. Our reactions seem to be automatically triggered by people and circumstances, and we forget that these are still choices that we are making in every moment of our existence. We are simply making these choices unconsciously."[17]

The Mind Field also transmits information coming from the collective consciousness. This means that we are subjected to the consensus reality which tells us how we are supposed to look and what is accepted or rejected by society. These thoughts seep in as judgments and criticism, which further tend to constrict the energy flow and accentuate the illusion of separateness and insecurity.

If we are ignorant as to the data contained in the files of our subconscious memory, we will simply find them reflected back to us in our Mind Field. The electromagnetic layer that surrounds us vibrates at a much faster velocity than our physical bodies. Therefore, the thoughts, feelings, and perceptions caught in the Field are constantly reproducing themselves in the experiences that they harvest.

Negative thoughts trapped in our mind fields tend to influence our perceptions of self, life, and the world.

44

Change Starts With You!

One of the more mature attitudes we can develop as healthy adults is to understand that we are incapable of changing anything or anybody outside of ourselves. Changing your external world is a fruitless endeavor. Once you make changes within your internal landscape, your outer world will alter, because what is vibrating out through your field will be different. People in your world will either change along with you, or they'll go away if they are not ready to deal with the new you. Learn this and you will save yourself a lot of useless expenditure of energy. Let me share some stories to illustrate this fact:

Hiroko is a talented artist and poet in Japan who has done much to promote the image of women in that country. She took my six-month course and experienced tremendous changes in her life. However, one major issue remained unresolved—she had experienced a falling out with her daughter almost 10 years before and from that time on had completely lost contact with her. This came up in a very emotional way one evening when the students had gone out for a few drinks after class. My co-teacher, Yuichi Nakajima, suggested that she communicate her deepest feelings to her daughter within a meditative state. He instructed her to let her daughter know on this internal level that she had forgiven her, and to seek forgiveness for any mistakes that she had made (see *Troubleshooting* – "Forgiveness Exercises" and "Creating the Safe Haven"). Amazingly, her daughter called her the very next day and suggested that they get together. In an emotional reunion, Hiroko met the grandchild she had never seen and re-established a more trusting and open relationship with her daughter!

Rebecca was trained as a biologist and had worked primarily in jobs that required complex, analytical thinking processes. She became interested in alternative therapies and began to study Reiki (a form of universal healing that originated in Japan and has been scientifically studied in the US). She loved this work so much that she decided to become a Master Practitioner, enabling her to train other individuals and activate their innate healing ability. However, she was reluctant to fully open up regarding her newfound spirituality with her husband of 16 years. Her concern was that he would not be receptive to these ideas. I suggested that she look within and face her own resistance. After all, with her intense scientific training, it was natural for her to wonder how others might view the concept of hands-on healing. Once she was clear with her own convictions, and had less fear about sharing her revelations, she began to notice a change in her husband. He even began to look forward to receiving Reiki sessions from her!

In both of these cases, the changes were instantaneous, proving once again, the power of thought. Once you make a commitment to change, without expecting that the other person make the first move, or heaping all the blame on them, you become a better person. In situations where there are long-held resentments, there will likely be the need to have some serious communication in order to resolve the issues, but an open heart and a positive attitude are magical potions to heal old wounds. The more you develop the flexibility to resist the old voices and behavioral patterns, the more space you will occupy in your subconscious and Mind Field. Then you become a serious player in the game of life.

The Superconscious Mind

There is yet another layer of the mind's structure that I would like to introduce you to: Meet your Superconscious Mind. Because of its transcendent and omniscient nature, the Superconscious Mind has also been called the Infinite Intelligence, the Higher Self, the Divine Essence, and the Inner Alchemist, among many others. Alchemy was the medieval chemistry of trying to turn base metals into gold. In esoteric terms, your Superconscious is the part of you that holds the vision of your highest potential – the gold of your true Self.

The Superconscious contains the seed of the place you are meant to fill in this world and no one else. It knows your mission on the planet, loves you unconditionally, and is willing to work as a collaborator on your path to self-realization. The Superconscious will not interfere unless asked to do so: your free will is never compromised. By aligning yourself with your Superconscious you open yourself to the experience of authentic power. The highest and most noble parts of yourself are within this part of your mind. Perhaps at times your Superconscious has made itself known to you by flashing across your mental screen visions or ideas that seemed improbable or unattainable to you, or appears as something that you'd describe as "too good to be true".[18] These are signals to you of how far your personal power can take you, once you learn to trust the guidance of your Higher Self. You can access your Superconscious through meditation, deep relaxation, prayer, and the altered state of consciousness known as hypnosis.

The Mind Field acts as a liaison to your Superconscious. While it remains polluted with fears and judgments, you are broadcasting an intention to remain in the state created by these negative thought forms. The SOS messages that you may be sending out to your Higher Self get distorted by the toxicity of your Field. As you liberate your Field of the constricting energy by becoming conscious of your subconscious material and clearing it, you send out waves of self-approval. These are returned to you by your Superconscious a hundred-fold. When your field becomes clearer it will seem to you that the clouds have parted and the sun is finally shining. The Superconscious bathes you in divine light, reminding you that you are always being protected. Your Infinite Intelligence has the capacity to get you through any situation and provide the wisdom and guidance you need to maneuver through life's maze.

Forgiveness

Not long ago I saw a wonderful interview on PBS with my favorite journalist, Bill Moyers and the Reverend Desmond Tutu, winner of the Nobel peace prize and major force in the disbanding of apartheid in South Africa. When asked how he could find forgiveness in the face of such atrocities to his people, Tutu replied "Forgiveness means that I am giving up my right to get even with you. By abandoning my claim to revenge, I do not let you victimize me by my holding on to the anger."

So much of our dynamic power is diffused in holding on to anger, resentments, and plotting our revenge. There is an ancient Chinese proverb that says "When you plan on doing revenge, you'd better dig two graves instead of one." As long as our energy remains trapped in the vicious cycle of retribution, we are more dead than alive.

A lack of forgiveness is recognized in mind/body medicine as being one of the most prolific causes in disease. Dr. Doreen Virtue, a psychotherapist who is well-know for her work with angels describes resentment in this way: "The anger you send outward acts like a laser beam pointed toward a mirror, and it instantly comes back and hits you." She advises that even if you don't feel ready to forgive someone's actions, then forgive the person instead. This single act can have a great healing effect on the world.[19]

Karen's story illustrates how once you let go of long-held resentments, life seems to open new doors to you:

I met Karen about a year ago. A neighbor of my closest friend, Karen would chat with me over coffee from time to time, and we began to develop our own friendship. She is from England and has a delightful sense of humor, is an admirable mother, and seems to be a fairly calm and well-balanced individual. One day as we were sharing our life histories she made a statement to me that I found quite shocking. She said, "You know, Linda, there are a couple people that I resent so deeply that I would be willing to do time to get even with them." Although I did not feel judgmental towards her, I was very impacted by the amount of toxic emotion that she was carrying inside. While I could empathize with how much she must have been hurt to have learned to hate so intensely, I was also aware of how much damage she was doing to herself and her loved ones with such poisonous thoughts. I couldn't imagine how this perfectly respectable citizen and mother would be willing to sacrifice her personal freedom and dignity for the sake of revenge. I allowed her the space to vent these emotions and asked if she was open to hearing my point of view, to which she agreed. I explained how the one that she was hurting the most was herself, as every thought finds its way back to us. Even if she succeeded in avenging herself with these individuals, in the long run, she would be doing herself greater harm.

As Karen was seeking a closer relationship with God through bible studies and more frequent church-going, I also suggested that these unresolved emotions could be holding her back from developing true spirituality. Finally, I speculated that such lethal feelings could be having a secondary effect on her loved ones. She agreed to practice forgiveness exercises every night before she went to bed. By understanding that she was not condoning the hurtful acts of these individuals, Karen was willing to sever the negative thought cords that were holding her back from her mental and spiritual growth.

She admitted to me that the first few nights she did more mental shouting at these people than forgiving, but by opening the channels to communication, she had begun the act of closure and release. Within a few nights she was sleeping more soundly and feeling as if a great load had lifted. It was not until three weeks later that she could mentally communicate with the gravest of her enemies without feeling tremendous rage. After this time she could actually carry on an imaginary conversation without any anger. Because she followed through with this commitment in spite of its great difficulty, within two months she was able to completely let go of any of the past hurts. In her words "It was like a pit in my stomach had healed and I felt physically lighter. I was carrying around a festering wound and now it's gone. I feel now that I am much more the person that I was meant to be. Even when I speak to my mother in England, she comments on how different I sound." Now, five months later, many things in her life have improved. Her relationship with her husband has experienced a renaissance and has brought them closer together. She also feels that this technique has become so ingrained in her mind, that she applies instant forgiveness to the things that happen throughout her active daily routine.

No matter what kind of resistance you have to the concept of forgiveness, I suggest you make the effort, even if you have to turn it over to your Superconscious mind or a Higher Power. Your power supply will greatly increase as will the manifestation of more positive experiences in your life. Zukav illustrates the process in this way: "When you release a negative thought, or a negative feeling, you release lower-frequency currents of energy from your system, and this literally, allows an increase in the frequency of your consciousness."[20]

Faith

When we face rejection, tragedy, loss, or challenging circumstances a natural conclusion is that perhaps we are being punished or singled out for suffering. With all of the negative images, critical voices and toxic thought forms already drifting through the Mind Field, it seems logical that we should react this way in the face of adversity. Yet we always have a choice as to how we can perceive a situation.

Faith is not a matter of believing – it is a knowingness that you are going to be okay in spite of very little tangible evidence in the present. Faith is acknowledging that there is a light at the end of a tunnel even if it only exists for the time being in your imagination. Without faith, we are prone to hopelessness and we lose our passion for life. However, if we can hold onto the vision of an eventual rescue or resolution, we are empowered and able to combat the overwhelming current of pessimistic thoughts. Faith is like a laser beam that can penetrate through the murkiness of the Mind Field and send a signal to your Superconscious that you are willing to change your perception of the situation.

Joan Borysenko, a well known lecturer in the field of mind/body medicine, teaches that crisis can pave the way for incredible healing providing that we are willing to hold on to the belief that we are suffering in the service of growth. She believes that "each wound we suffer and eventually heal from is a soul-making experience with the potential to awaken our willingness to participate in the healing of our world."[21]

Viktor Frankl, the author of *Man's Search for Meaning* and creator of logotherapy, suffered inconceivable losses in a concentration camp during World War II. He lost his parents, wife, children, reputation, home, and belongings, yet he retained his dignity by understanding that man always has the choice on how he perceives adversity. His unwavering faith allowed him to turn a personal tragedy into a triumph.[22]

I used to play the "what if" game with my clients, inviting them to consider the possibility that unfortunate circumstances in their lives may really be a kind of message or invitation to take a different path. If you can for a few moments accept the premise that we live in a benevolent universe, contemplate on how the sufferings that you have gone through may have been to awaken you or nudge you towards another direction.

Marianne Williamson, the compelling authority on *A Course in Miracles,* characterizes faith as "believing that the universe is on our side, and that the universe knows what it's doing. Faith is a psychological awareness of an unfolding force for good, constantly at work in all dimensions".[23]

Intuition

Intuition means to be tutored from within. In its role as our inner guide, the Superconscious continuously sends us signals, clues, and messages to help us make decisions congruent with our higher purpose. These messages may not be obvious to us at first as they are caught up in the noise and chaos of our busy Mind Field. In fact, until we learn to trust this guidance, we have a tendency to ignore it or override it with our "logic". Most westernized cultures are not accustomed to take internal communication or intuition seriously, because it has become equated with being psychic or mentally unbalanced.

The Superconscious has tremendous respect for the fact that all decisions must ultimately be generated by your free will. It merely points the way through subtle clues or even in-your-face revelations. If you are willing to enlist your Superconscious as your advisor, your guidance will come by means of intuition. Answers will appear to you as hunches, a chance remark, a passage in a book that suddenly leaps out to you, or even in the words to a song that suddenly comes through on the radio.

I remember a time in my life when I was feeling very alone and bordering on a deep depression. I knew that it was only a matter of time before I would become incapable of functioning in my practice, because it seemed a lot more appealing to me to stay home in bed than go into the clinic. As I was driving to my office and feeling very low, I said out loud that I was ready to "see" the situation in a new light and that I was willing to surrender to whatever changes needed to take place in my life. A moment later a song came on the radio that seemed to speak to me directly, telling me that I was not alone and that things would turn out okay. In that transcendent moment my spirits lifted instantly and I felt that I could make it through the dark times.

The more we clear our subconscious mind of belief systems that

51

chastise us and perpetuate our insecurity, the more open we become to the guidance of our Superconscious mind. When you learn to trust your intuition, you no longer feel paralyzed by choice and decision-making because somehow you sense which road to take. You can release the out-dated and limiting beliefs that cloud your Mind Field via the hypnotic state.

If reality is created through our thoughts, then it would stand to reason that a mind that produces and acknowledges more positive thoughts than negative thoughts will manifest a brighter and happier existence.

Hypnosis

While suggestion is the motivating force to spur the subconscious into action, we are much more receptive to suggestion while in the hypnotic state. In other words, we are continually open to suggestion, however, being in hypnosis takes us further along the suggestibility scale.

We tend to think of hypnosis as an extraordinary state, induced by some outside force or agent. Yet, hypnosis is a very natural and ordinary state; in fact, we drift in and out of this state about a dozen times a day without taking particular notice. Whenever we are focused inward and less receptive to outside stimuli we are entering the altered state of the mind called hypnosis. This state is when the subconscious mind temporarily shifts into the dominant position. Bradshaw, who has done amazing work with family systems and healing the inner child, says that "most of us go in and out of trance many times during the course of the day. We daydream, we get absorbed in future fantasies, we relive old memories from the past."[24]

Any altered state of consciousness can be considered hypnosis, although the level of trance may vary. The brain wave pattern of the alert conscious state for most of our daily routines is called *beta*. When we start to detach from outside stimuli, such as when we daydream, this is called *alpha*. Deeper states of trance and the stage of sleep in which we dream the most is called *theta*. The deepest states of hypnosis and dreamless sleep produce *delta* waves. Hypnosis, with its varying degrees of depth, is associated with *alpha, theta,* and *delta.* Dr. Winifred Blake Lucas, a board diplomat in psychology and long time professor at UCLA, used brain wave detectors while working with trance subjects experiencing childhood and past live regressions. She found that the brain wave patterns would waver between these three states throughout the session, but greatest amount of recall was evoked while in the *delta* state. Therefore, in any level of hypnosis—light, medium, or deep— the subconscious is receptive to suggestion.

The exposure that most individuals have to hypnosis comes through either stage shows or some kind of cartoon or movie that revolves around the theme. These situations give a rather distorted view and tend to provoke fear, distrust or amusement without allowing for hypnosis to be considered as a science and viable therapeutic modality. The treatment of hypnosis by Hollywood is generally that of mind control, featuring a kind of Svengali figure who virtually dominates the mind of his subject and manipulates him to commit some kind of heinous crime. This is complete fiction since there is not one documented case in which it has been proven that an individual would be obliged to do something against their will while in the hypnotic state. Unfortunately, ignorance of the subject by moviemakers has caused some serious damage to the image of the hypnotherapist and discourages many from considering treatment because of these unsubstantiated fears.

The image presented in the night club type of hypnosis show is very detrimental. I'm sure that at some time you have seen one of these, either on the television, in an amusement park or nightclub act. Subjets are invited from the audience and choosen carefully to ensure maximum participation and effect. It has been estimated that approximately 30% of the population will rapidly go into the deepest states of hypnosis; certainly, they are the preferable candidates for a stage performance, as they will readily comply with the most complex suggestions and skits. The audience is then entertained and astounded by the seemingly ridiculous situations that the hypnotized subject willingly carries out, convincing the audience that the hypnotist is either a wizard or that the volunteer has been pre-chosen in order to dupe them. Neither of these scenarios is true, nor are they necessary. The hypnotist (at this point I will refrain from referring to him or her as a hypnotherapist as many of them are more committed to the use of hypnosis for fascination and amusement purposes rather than for helping humanity) is well aware that in the hypnotic state the subconscious mind becomes dominant. Certain phenomena (which will be explained in depth later in this chapter) are then immediately accessible, because the subconscious is in the dominant position. In the normal, everyday conscious state of awareness these marvels are not as readily available. These phenomena are God-given gifts that can enable us to discover more of our inner potential and facilitate learning and growth. Yet, the stage performer generally vulgarizes these gifts for the sole purpose of entertainment and self-aggrandizement.

The image presented in stage show hypnosis is very misleading

In all fairness I must admit that I have occasionally seen a stage hypnotist use his or her show as a vehicle for educating and informing their audience on the many benefits of using hypnosis therapeutically. One show that I attended at Magic Mountain amusement park in Southern California several years ago so impressed me that I stayed after the show to compliment the hypnotist. Yet, last year I attended another show at the same place with another hypnotist that was so disturbing that I left mid-way, extremely disgusted with the treatment of the volunteers. A friend who had accompanied me was totally turned off to hypnosis because of this spectacle, which only emphasizes the point I'm tying to make. Although a stage show can be great fun and can be used as a means of demonstrating the vast resources of the mind and the clinical applications of hypnosis, for the most part they ridicule the participants and belittle the science. In my opinion, the majority of the audience will leave these types of shows with the conviction that hypnosis is either dangerous or foolish. And were they to be in need of therapy the last modality they would consider would be hypnosis for fear that they would be manipulated or made to perform some foolish act.

A lack of awareness to the nature of the hypnotic state and the exceptional benefits that can be obtained from using it in an intentional manner, is not limited to the uneducated or naïve. Education and sophistication do not guarantee that one has been exposed to the reality of this science. For example, my former gynecologist, a brilliant and well-traveled man, would take off his watch and slowly wave it back and forth before my eyes on my yearly examinations in a parody of the typical representations that I have outlined above. Yet, the Lamaze method of natural childbirth uses deep breathing and guided relaxation techniques which are quite clearly hypnotic inductions. If obstetricians were educated in the proper use of suggestion and the elaboration of the hypnotic phenomena, many women could experience a virtually painless childbirth!

Intentional vs. Unintentional Hypnosis

As you go through your normal daily activities, your blood circulates through your veins, your food is digested and assimilated, your heart continues to beat, and you breathe air into your lungs; ultimately, you perform these processes automatically and without awareness or conscious effort on your part. At the same time, your mind is going through a natural process in which power and attention are shifting from conscious to subconscious functions. This, too, goes on without any conscious effort or any particular awareness of this shift.

Thus, the dance of dominance between the conscious and subconscious is a natural rhythm which can be likened to balancing scales. During most of our ordinary and normal daily events, the conscious mind retains the dominant position. About a dozen times a day, however, the subconscious mind takes over. When the subconscious mind is dominant, this state can be referred to as the common everyday trance. Here are some examples of this state:

• You are driving home from work. Suddenly you pull into your driveway and realize you've been so lost in thought that you don't even remember the last few blocks or how you got there.

• You are so completely absorbed in the drama on the television program you're watching, that you jump when someone touches you to get your attention.

• You are in a long, tedious meeting. Your mind starts to drift and you daydream about the trip you want to take to Europe next year.

• You are lying on the couch listening to a CD. The music begins to draw you in, and you find yourself reliving a past moment in your life. You feel emotion welling up inside you and might even feel an urge to weep.

• You are listening to a relaxation tape or participating in a meditative process.

All of these are examples of *unintentional states of hypnosis.* It may surprise you to learn that you have been hypnotized so often and under such ordinary conditions that you never knew anything about it! This happens simply because you have been led to believe that hypnosis is an extraordinary state—produced by magic or mind control—which is certainly not the case.

Dr. Ernest Rossi discovered a natural mind-body rhythm occurring in us every 90 to 120 minutes. These mental and physiological cycles, called Ultradian Rhythms are equated to REM (rapid eye movement) periods of sleep, but are also duplicated in the waking state. Unlike the circadian rhythm (regulating sleep and wakefulness), which occurs once every twenty-four hours, the Ultradians occur over a dozen times a day, every day of our lives. During these biological cycles, which last approximately 20 minutes, we have more of a mind/body connection and are prone more to daydreaming and fantasy. This would suggest that the subconscious mind is more dominant during these periods, making them *unintentional states of hypnosis.* Rossi refers to this phenomenon as the Ultradian Healing Response and theorizes that when we learn to recognize these occurrences, they can be used dynamically to interpret messages from the body, relieve accumulated tension, rejuvenate, facilitate natural healing, and explore creative insights.[25]

Unintentional hypnosis is also produced spontaneously whenever we are exposed to a traumatic or stressful situation. This causes the critical factor to step aside as soon as the fight or flight syndrome begins to manifest itself, allowing the subconscious mind to come into the dominant position. If you have ever been highly stressed, had a panic attack, been in shock, or suffered from a serious illness, you have experienced *unintentional hypnosis.* Most likely, considering the intensity of modern life, this is something that you may experience almost on a daily basis!

Michael Preston, Ph.D., an expert in the field of medical hypnosis, believes that eighty percent of our problems have their origin in unintentional hypnosis. Because the unconscious mind is so receptive during these periods, we are virtually shoveling in all our negative thoughts, images, and perceptions. The subconscious then acts upon these suggestions, turning all of those self-sabotaging suggestions into self-fulfilling prophecies.

Anything that we do by rote or second nature also allows the critical factor of the mind to take a break and the subconscious to rise into dominance. While driving, washing the dishes, or performing any activity without having to analyze or maintain constant awareness, we are also receptive to suggestion. All of these actions naturally tip the scales to subconscious dominance.

What this means for you: If you were to catch yourself in those moments of daydreaming, stressing out, driving, and performing mundane activities by rote and stopped to analyze your thoughts, what would the majority of those thoughts center on? More than likely, the main themes would be what you desire or what you feel that you are lacking. Thoughts like:

Life is so difficult. I have such bad luck. Nobody loves me. If only

I could have this, I'd be so happy. I'm getting old. I'm too fat. Today's just not my day.

Your subconscious is listening and acting upon those suggestions. This has a lot to do with your not getting what you *consciously* want. But you are indeed getting what you *unconsciously* ask for!

Hypnosis by *intention,* on the other hand, is when you consciously seek to produce the trance state. The subjects that we see being hypnotized on stage are being *intentionally* hypnotized. However, sometimes there are people sitting in the audience who enter the trance without having consciously participated in the induction. This is *unintentional* hypnosis.

When you focus your awareness on your breath or systematically relax every muscle in your body, listen to relaxation or meditation tapes, practice self-hypnosis, or go to a hypnotherapist you are practicing *intentional hypnosis.* It is through intentional hypnosis (also known as self-hypnosis) that you can counteract the results of the negative programming that you unwittingly accepted and implanted throughout your life.

In the normal waking state, the conscious mind is dominant.

As many as a dozen times a day the subconscious comes into dominance, creating the unintentional state of hypnosis.

The Treasures in Your Subconscious

Once the subconscious makes the shift to the dominant position, we have access to the hypnotic phenomena that I have described as *expanded faculties* of this larger portion of our minds. Stage hypnotists draw upon these capacities in order to mesmerize their audience, but with informed knowledge of these gifts, you can purposely adapt them toward improving your life experience. What you may have considered to be impossible or beyond your capacities up to now, can easily be activated once you practice intentional states of hypnosis! Imagine being able to bring forth dynamic aspects of your personality effortlessly, controlling pain with your mind or expanding and contracting time according to your needs. All of these seemingly magical abilities are just beyond your conscious awareness.

There have been times when these phenomena have been activated within unintentional hypnosis without you being aware that you were in an altered state.

SCENARIO: You are walking barefoot on a beach at sunset, arm in arm with a loved one completely enraptured by their company and the beauty of your surroundings. You feel a slight pinch on your left foot, but it is barely noticeable and you keep walking, totally within the moment. The sun slips gently into the ocean. Sometime later you return to your room and notice:

a) The sole of your left foot has been cut, perhaps by a sharp rock or a piece of broken glass. While not serious, this was still a substantial cut and you are surprised that you felt no pain when it happened.

b) The two of you had been walking and talking on the beach for more than two hours and you had estimated that you had been there for less than a half hour!

Being so involved in the present and open within all of your senses is an altered state of consciousness, a positive unintentional hypnotic state in which the subconscious yields its treasures.

Myths and Misconceptions

Let's clear up some myths and misconceptions regarding hypnosis. Because of the totally inappropriate way that hypnosis has been depicted, you may have certain belief systems that would interfere with taking advantage of this valuable healing modality.

First of all, hypnosis is not sleep. Although a hypnotized subject gives the appearance of being asleep and a hypnotherapist may even use the words "deep sleep" in order to more fully relax the subject, hypnosis resembles the waking state much more than the sleeping state. Research laboratories have found the EEG patterns (measuring brain wave activity) to be distinctly different than those of the sleep state. In a physical examination, when the doctor hits your knee with the rubber hammer this is what is known as the patellar reflex. If you are awake or hypnotized when given this test, the bottom part of your leg will respond with a swift kick upwards, but while sleeping there will be no response. If you are listening to your guided meditation tape while in bed at night you may fall asleep, but this is not hypnosis, it just means that you are tired and fell asleep; however, in the early stages of sleep your subconscious still receives most of the suggestions.

Another common misrepresentation of hypnosis is that it is a state of unconsciousness. The word "trance", for example, has come to mean some kind of zombie-like state in which a person has no control over his or her actions. This cannot be farther from the truth. Hypnosis so much resembles the waking state that an individual is aware of any interior or exterior movement or noise, but is usually quite focused and relaxed. The mind can be quite active during the trance state. Hypnosis is not at all like being under anesthesia. In fact, I usually avoid the term "under hypnosis" because it is a pejorative term, which implies that the subject is under the control of the therapist. The hypnotherapist holds no power whatsoever over the subject and cannot force them to do something against their will or against their morals. There's nothing magical about hypnosis. It is a natural state that we drift in and out of many times a day, such as when we daydream; get lost in thought driving, unable to recall the last few miles we've just driven; or even when we are in deep meditation or prayer. An easy way to describe this is as an in-between state: A state between being awake and being asleep. The only thing magical about this state is that it links you directly to your subconscious mind and all the potential contained therein.

What is really vital for the readers to understand is that *all hypnosis is self-hypnosis!* Hypnosis is a natural state and not something that is being done *to* us. When we experience hypnosis by means of a hypnotherapist or an induction cassette, we are simply being guided into this state—not forced to do something against our will or without our consent. In the *Tool Kit* section of this book I will cover the actual dynamics of suggestion as well as other means for reprogramming, but I would like to emphasize that self-hypnosis facilitates a direct communication to the subconscious and allows you to fully relax at the same time.

Let's examine how an unscrupulous hypnotist can misrepresent the hypnotic phenomena, and how they can be developed either in a clinical situation or as part of your self-hypnosis program.

Rapid Body and Temperature Changes

The stage hypnotist yells "Sleep!" and the chins of all the seated subjects drop to their chests, their arms flop at their sides and some of them seem to start slumping in their chairs. Next, the hypnotist suggests to his subjects that they have been stranded in a blizzard in sub-zero temperatures. They start to shiver and seek each other out for heat until they receive the next suggestion, advising them that they are in a nice, warm room. Now, once again, everyone is relaxed and comfortable. Have they been converted into robots? Are these magical powers at work? Not at all.

The hypnotic (subconscious-dominant) state promotes the rapid acceptance of suggestion and immediately accesses the involuntary physical processes of the body, as you learned in Part I. There is also a general absence of critical reasoning, which explains the willingness of the subjects. Muscles can quickly expand and contract, facilitating relaxation. However, it is important here to emphasize that the subject can override any suggestion by an act of volition. Generally, the subconscious *willingly* follows any suggestion that is not detrimental to its physical well being and is not morally objectionable.

What this means for you: We live in an era of *stress* – one of the major buzzwords of our generation. It is also no secret that stress has a lot to do with our lowered immune response and susceptibility to disease. While the pat advice "you've got to calm down" or "try to relax" is sage, it's not something that we can accomplish through conscious intent. Remember the *Law of Concentrated Attention*? Stress becomes habitual through repeated focus on feeling anxious, nervous or uptight. Once that pattern becomes entrenched in our subconscious, it can only be counter-reacted through suggestions that promote calm and tranquility.

When you use intentional states of hypnosis, whether it is through guided meditation, progressive relaxation, self-hypnosis, listening to specialized tapes or experiencing a session with a therapist, your subconscious responds instantly to suggestions, releasing stored tension in the specified muscle groups. Relaxation is perhaps the greatest benefit of using altered states when you consider how vital it is for our bodies to maintain homeostasis in order to function optimally.

If I were to ask you now, as you read these words, to voluntarily raise your body temperature by two degrees you would probably not be able to accomplish this without the use of altered states. The critical factor of your conscious mind blocks access to the part of your psyche that controls body temperature, respiration, circulation, blood pressure, etc. The great yogis of India have been known to survive for long periods in extreme temperatures without any clothing, have walked on burning coals and swallowed fire. What we have observed as bizarre and unexplainable is quite understandable when we consider the yogis' dominion over the unconscious mind.[26]

One of the greatest teachers of yogis, Pantajali, described yoga and meditation as the process of cleansing the movements arising from the subconscious mind.[27] Disciples of meditation have been trained to spend hours in the meditative state, which is virtually a passive form of hypnosis. Through countless hours of observation and detachment from your subconscious content, it is indeed possible to purify your subconscious debris. Yet with the application of intentional hypnosis you can accomplish a great deal in a short time. My own yoga teacher, Marshall Govindan, has often referred individuals to me whom, in spite of their devoted practice of yoga and meditation, have encountered subconscious blocks. He believes that it is vital to consciously examine the origins of our belief systems through the tools of hypnosis. This then enables us to advance on our spiritual path.

In the *Tool Kit* and *Troubleshooting* sections of this guide you will learn techniques for relaxation, voluntary muscle control, pain control and healing.

Limb Catalepsy

Limb Catalepsy is a classic routine employed by the old-timers. The hypnotist places a female subject in a trance and suspends her head and feet between two chairs with no central support. He then stands on her mid-section, demonstrating how the body remains rigid instead of collapsing under his weight. Not only is it dangerous to the subject to have excess weight heaped upon her vital organs, this spectacle is also one of the most superfluous demonstrations of the benefits of hypnosis. This parody is also somewhat deceiving as it leads us to believe that the hypnotist has some mystical power. What is really at play here is the survival instinct. If you were placed between two chairs, your body would stiffen in an effort to protect it from falling. It's as simple as that.

Does limb catalepsy exist then? Absolutely. The same occurrence when a suggestion is given to relax a muscle can cause rigidity. While there is no clear clinical use for this state, systematically tensing and then relaxing a muscle will increase the release of anxiety. Hypnotherapists use limb catalepsy as what is called a *convincer* or a *suggestibility test* in order to prove to the client that their subconscious is indeed responding to suggestions. This alerts the client that they are in an altered state and enhances the spiral of belief that allows for more sophisticated applications of hypnosis to be implemented.

Hypno-Anesthesia

A suggestion is made to the subject that a part of his or her body is becoming numb and impervious to pain. Then the hypnotist, with no medical training or license, proceeds to insert a large needle into the subject's gum or through their skin. The sad thing here, is that instead of illustrating the fantastic ability that we have to alter or block pain, the observer of such a show is turned off or frightened. This crude display does not allow us to make the connection that we can use this marvelous skill ourselves. Whenever I see this phenomenon demonstrated by an unprincipled stage performer I become extremely incensed due to the residual fear it can incite

We are so primed to put our power outside of ourselves, looking for some pill, miracle cure or healer, yet this phenomenon requires only a light to medium altered state and is one of the easiest to carry out. For demonstration purposes you can create quite an impression on your audience by a simple pinprick or pinch test.

While it is possible for a hypnotherapist to create anesthesia or analgesia in any part of the client's body by means of direct suggestion, what I most support is training the client to re-create this state themselves. This way they can treat chronic pain as needed without being dependent on the therapist. First of all, it is imperative that the therapist determine if a medical doctor has treated the pain or symptom. Pain is a signal that something is wrong. Removing the pain may remove the motivation of the client to get the proper medical attention. However, when it has been determined that nothing more can be done but learning to live with chronic pain or depending on a prescription or over-the-counter analgesic, this is the ideal time to resort to *hypno-anesthesia*.

The most popular method is called *glove anesthesia*. The numbness or insensitivity is localized in the dominant hand (or whichever one is more accessible to the area of chronic pain) and then transferred to the affected body part, thereby removing any discomfort for four to eight hours. The client is then taught how to do this through their personal self-hypnosis.

What this means for you: This is a simple procedure that you can create through self-hypnosis (see *Troubleshooting*), eliminating the need for analgesics and painkillers that produce dependency and side effects. You are also prepared in an emergency situation to help yourself deal with injuries and pain.

Personality Changes

The hypnotized subject is given a suggestion that he is Michael Jackson doing the moon dance, or one of the Spice Girls on tour. This personality change is certainly amusing to the audience, but here again, the crucial message is lost in the absurd. Once the critical factor is bypassed, so are many of the conscious mind's inhibitions and limitations. As observers we often wonder how the subjects can make such fools of themselves, but again, it is important to realize that they are *not* being coerced to act against their will. To a certain degree they are having a liberating experience which, in other circumstances, would probably serve them well in their search for self-improvement. But in the stage show venue they are often ridiculed by the hypnotist and their peers, which can leave a residual effect, even to the point of creating or exacerbating complexes. As a professional hypnotherapist who uses the science as a way of helping people heal their complexes and improve their self- image, I find this distressing.

What this means for you: Perhaps you perceive yourself as a shy person, or someone who is not particularly creative. Your self-image is based largely on the "picture" of you that is generated through your conscious mind. Your critical factor is constantly communicating the limitations of your Self and inhibiting you from discovering the vast potential locked in your subconscious mind. In these deeper regions of the subconscious mind there are a myriad of choices—many alter egos and sub-personalities that can be brought into action, as they are needed.

For instance, let's say that you are scheduled to give a talk in front of a group of colleagues and the idea of speaking in public terrifies you. As you've already learned from the *Law of Reverse Effect*, to try to override that fear by sheer will power is not going to work. By using intentional states of hypnosis you can suggest that the part or parts of you that are more extroverted, dynamic and confident to rehearse the speech for you while you are in the altered state. This practice will expand your critical factor's perception of you and at the appointed time of your speech you will be amazed at how much more prepared you feel.

The phenomenon of personality changes can let you "try on" many new aspects of Self, so that you become more expansive and well rounded.

Positive and Negative Hallucinations

In the hypnotic state our imagination is virtually unlimited. We are able to alter our perception of reality and create mirages that seem very real to us. Let me clarify here that when referring to hallucinations as being positive or negative, this is **not** a value judgement as to whether they are good or bad. A positive hallucination is the creation of an illusion through any of the five senses: visual, auditory, touch, taste, and smell. For example, we have seen hypnotized subject's on stage petting a cat in their lap that is invisible to our eyes, or laughing at a comedy that exists only in the imagination. This is what we call a positive hallucination – something created in the imagination through the five senses.

A negative hallucination is the withdrawal of a sensory stimulus from the subject's awareness. A classic and amusing routine is having a subject "see" the audience completely naked. Naturally, no one has removed any clothing, but the hypnotized individual would hallucinate everyone as nude. This is what we call a negative hallucination – the illusion that something is not there, even if it is. The negative hallucination generally is more difficult to produce than the positive, so hypnotists use only those subjects for these routines that have proved to be the most cooperative and appear to be in a deeper trance.

What this means for you: As I have emphasized earlier in this chapter, thought is the magnetic force that attracts experience to you and creates your reality. Through the *Law of Concentrated Attention* you bring to you what you have focused your energy upon. By applying visualization and imagery to your thoughts, meditations, suggestions, prayers and daydreams you are super-charging the laser beam and intensifying the magnetic force.

In this technological age of virtual reality and sophisticated special effects, our innate imaginative capacity has somewhat diminished, like a muscle that becomes weakened through disuse. You can enhance your inner vision when you utilize positive and negative hallucinations in the altered state. Positive hallucinations will expand your guided imagery. Negative hallucinations will help you deal with unpleasant realities. For instance, if you need to take a certain supplement or medicine and can't tolerate the taste, you can alter the flavor to make it more palatable.

Focusing your attention on an idea, thought, feeling or concept is like shining a laser beam on it, magnifying the intensity.

In the *Tool Kit* section you will learn that not all of us use our imagination in the same way, nor do we process information through the same channels. Some people tend to get an automatic image, while others record data in a more sensory way, such as how something impacted them emotionally. With the tools, surveys, and exercises provided you too can super-charge your imagination and activate more of the dormant treasures in your subconscious mind.

Post-Hypnotic Suggestions

Post-hypnotic suggestions are cues that continue to function even when the subject has returned to normal consciousness. On the stage a subject is told that upon "awakening" every time the hypnotist taps their chin or rings a bell they are to jump up and sing the national anthem or dance the polka. When confronted with their strange behavior, the subject is likely to give what seems to them to be a rational explanation. Even if the hypnotist were to forget to remove the non-therapeutic post-hypnotic suggestion it would automatically disappear or be dreamed out within seventy-two hours.

Post-hypnotics do not have to be silly. In fact they are quite potent when directed towards dealing with stress, habitual behavior and healing because they are working outside the hypnotherapist's office. Hundreds of clients in years of clinical practice were able to successfully deal with anxiety through the application of a post-hypnotic suggestion in which they would automatically open and close a fist when stressed out, silently or verbally pronouncing the word "control". This suggestion would eventually break the stressor circuit in the program stored in the autonomic nervous system. Soon the client was no longer at the mercy of an automatic reaction to a stressful situation, such as pressure at work or traffic delays because the subconscious was no longer programmed that way. You will find this therapeutic technique, as well as others in *Troubleshooting*.

What this means for you: In the altered state you can give yourself suggestions that will continue to work even while in the conscious state. For example, you can tell yourself that every time you open a file drawer you associate that action with filing away any of the problems or issues that have been troubling you. Or, that as you reach over to turn off the lamp on your night table, you yawn deeply and prepare to enter a luxurious and restful sleep. If you are trying to lose weight, you can suggest that when you approach the refrigerator door between meals you have a sense of fullness and satisfaction in your stomach. Post–hypnotics are excellent bridges to make your conscious awareness more productive.

Amnesia and Hypermnesia

We've all seen this one. A subject is told to forget their name or a number temporarily. The hypnotist then has great fun at the subject's expense trying to get them to count to ten minus that digit or pronounce their name. This is one of the most senseless and misleading of all the phenomena we've examined so far. Blocking information from the subconscious is called **amnesia** and it gives the impression that the hypnotist has the power to erase data from the mind. I can't even begin to estimate how many jilted lovers have called me over the years, begging for some sort of treatment to make them instantly forget an ex-boyfriend or girlfriend. This is a giant misconception. Nothing that has been recorded upon the subconscious can be erased. It can be temporarily blocked, but it will not disappear permanently. In fact, there is very little clinical use for the phenomenon of amnesia. Blocking emotionally painful information can be dangerous because there is no guarantee that should it suddenly become nudged into awareness, that someone will be there to help the subject cope.

Hypermnesia on the other hand is a very valuable tool. The opposite of amnesia, hypermnesia is what we call "enhanced memory". As I mentioned above, nothing that has ever been recorded by the five senses upon the cerebral cortex of the brain as a memory can ever be voluntarily erased. (An exception to this would be in the case of severe organic brain damage caused by a cerebral hemorrhage or an accident) Therefore, the subconscious retains the memory of everything that has ever happened to us. Some law enforcement agencies elicit information from witnesses using the hypnotic state and hypermnesia.

As a specialist in regression therapy, I have taken thousands of indi-

69

viduals back to significant moments in their lifetimes to uncover the source of the identifications and negative perceptions that have shaped their self and world view. As we become conscious of the painful events that formed these damaging self-opinions, we are able to offer them up for healing and achieve a higher perspective of our life purpose.

Many therapists around the world are using regression therapy to take clients back to past lives. This would seem to imply a belief in reincarnation, but I am reluctant to impose this belief system on anyone who would find it to be at odds with their particular religious upbringing. In consideration of the many different cultures I work with, the best way to approach a past life regression is to consider it a metaphor, or a teaching tale offered by your Superconscious mind in its infinite wisdom with the purpose of healing you or enlightening you on a certain issue.

What this means for you: If you would like to experience regression, I recommend that you seek out a competent hypnotherapist or psychologist trained in these techniques. If you attempt to do a self-regression, powerful emotions could surface that you may not know how to address on your own. These are called *abreactions* – overwhelming reactions to suppressed material in the subconscious.

However, you can use hypermnesia as part of your self-hypnosis to expand your own recall and concentration. Books such as Sheila Ostrander's *Super Learning* and *Super Memory* reveal many techniques in which memory and concentration can be enhanced through the use of altered states.

Another clinical use for hypermnesia is for finding lost or misplaced objects. While in trance, take yourself back in time, step by step to the last time that you saw the object. Then suggest that you go to the point right before it was lost and you will be amazed to find that valuable ring in a place you hadn't even searched! One of my more memorable cases was helping a woman recall the numbers to a Swiss bank account that her family had during the war to protect their assets. In the hypnotic state she was able to bring forth numbers that she hadn't known or used for twenty-five years!

Time Distortion

The use of time distortion is not commonly employed by hypnotists for stage shows; however, I chose to include it because of its merit. The subconscious mind does not function linearly, and therefore is not bound by the same concept of time and space as is the conscious mind. For this reason, subjects in a regression can retrieve memories from the past with exceptional detail and feel as if they were actually reliving the moment.

We have all found ourselves reliving moments when time seemed to pass instantly, as in the beach scenario at the beginning of this chapter. This usually occurs when we were doing something that we love or are totally absorbed in at the moment. In other situations time seems to drag on, making the day seem endless. This tends to support the concept that time is an illusion – a consensus reality that has been agreed upon as a way of measuring our days.

What this means for you: The phenomenon of time distortion can be used to expand or contract time according to your needs. I have worked with pregnant women prior to their due date and in the delivery room where they were primed through post-hypnotic suggestions to experience a minute-long contraction as lasting only five seconds!

You can make your workday fly by—or you can make eight hours seem like 16 and get twice as much accomplished. You can also compress a full night's sleep into just a few hours and receive the same benefits as if you had experienced the long rest. Try some of these examples yourself once you become proficient with the self-hypnosis methods supplied in your *Tool Kit.*

Part III: Tool Kit

People don't usually lack resources:
they lack control over their resources.

Anthony Robbins

₁₀ Use Your Tool Kit

Your *Tool Kit* functions as a workbook with exercises, self-tests, guided meditations, and visualizations, as well a lot of food for thought. Having the following items on hand will assure your getting the most out of this section: a pen or pencil, a notebook or loose paper, a tape recorder (optional), and some soothing music.

There are several processes and inductions included in this section to guide you into the trance state; below are some recommendations on how you can optimize your experiences:

A) After choosing a technique you'd like to try, read through it several times and then go through it mentally from memory. It's not important that you follow it to the letter, so feel free to modify any of the inductions to suit your needs.

B) Record the induction on one side of a 60-minute tape, either in your own voice or ask someone whose voice you resonate with to record it for you. If you are doing the recording for yourself make sure to *speak slowly*. It's probably best that you practice reading through the entire script once or twice before you start. The art of the hypnotic voice is to speak slowly and use your voice to express what the word is saying. For instance, the word *deep* is much more effective when you actually deepen your own voice. You may be surprised to find that you have your own unique hypnotic style. Try out various styles, such as maternal (as if you were speaking a lullaby to a child); sweet (being very loving and compassionate); sensual (a romantic touch) or even a monotone which will lull you into a comfortable altered state. What is particularly effective for heightening the relaxation, as well as pacing the speed of your voice, is to play soothing music in the background, such as light classical pieces or nature sounds. You may want to explore the new age section of your local music store as this type of music is especially designed for meditation and stress reduction. Steve Halpern is a renowned artist in this field and almost all of his CD's or audiocassettes will enhance the experience.

It is also very important that in recording your own tape in your own voice, you convert the suggestions to first person. Every time you see the word *you* replace it with *I,* and when you see the word *your*, replace it with *my*. Although it is quite effective to receive hypnotic suggestion from someone else, giving yourself the suggestions (self-hypnosis) is **three times more powerful**! Remember, you are the architect of your destiny. When having someone else record the meditation it is best that they use the pronouns *you* and *yours*.

C) If you do not choose to make a tape, you can have someone read the induction to you out loud and *slowly*. Follow the instructions above.

D) If you would feel more comfortable with a professionally recorded tape, see the order form in the back of the book. Most of the hypnotic exercises in your *Tool Kit* and *Troubleshooting* section are available individually or as a series.

You may practice your inductions or listen to your tape either sitting down or lying down in a comfortable position. If you are lying in bed you may very well fall asleep, but you will still receive the benefits of the suggestions. You can even put the tape on at bedtime, however, do try to work with the processes during the day or when you are most alert to ensure the best results. It is advisable that you are in a place where you will be uninterrupted for the length of the induction. If you find that you must terminate the induction or the process before the end, make sure that you give yourself a few moments to assimilate the experience before you resume normal activities. *Under no circumstances should you listen to any hypnotic cassette while driving an automobile or while operating any machinery.*

I Love Me—I Love Me Not

According to many child psychologists, a critical factor in the development of self-esteem is unconditional parental approval and acceptance. In the absence of a healthy childhood it is considered to be quite difficult to change one's level of worthiness in an upward direction.[28] Self-esteem is the way one feels about oneself. It is the barometer of how competent we feel in the world as opposed to a sense of inadequacy. When we have a functional self-esteem we have more self-respect and acceptance and tend to perceive ourselves through our strengths rather than our weaknesses. Without the positive foundation that teaches us high regard for self, we are often plagued with feelings of inferiority. We compare ourselves unfavorably with others or struggle to achieve approval.

Think about the people whom you admire the most. They are the ones who seem to take good care of themselves and display high levels of discipline and ambition. They are active and successful. They look healthy and seem to enjoy their lives. In fact, you probably think they have some kind of lucky star guiding their lives that somehow passed you by. Maybe some of these individuals had the blessing of a good childhood which guided them into the right careers or provided them with the proper environment for success. However, not all successful people were raised to have a high regard for self. Many of these individuals had to struggle against incredible odds to overcome debilitating programming, developing self-esteem in the process. In other words, even if you did not have a fairy tale childhood, you can learn to love yourself!

To set a goal for higher self-esteem is a noble one, but rather unspecific. Self-love, or the lack thereof, can be broken down into smaller components. To undertake the task of loving ourselves is a lifelong project, and we need to take some baby steps before we can leap and run.

A couple of years ago, Japan Medical Arts—the company that promotes me in Japan—asked me to put a course together on self-hypnosis. Although the majority of my international work involves training hypnotherapists, they suggested that learning the tools of self-hypnosis might be useful to their mainstream clientele for improving the quality of their lives and dealing with the high stress levels of life in busy Tokyo. Although my day and a half format was presented to them with the title "Self-Hypnosis for Mind/Body/Spirit Integration", by the time the course description was translated and advertised in their catalogue, the title was changed to "I Love Me" on the suggestion of the president of the company. The response to this course was enthusiastic and we received a lot of feedback from the participants that the title was one of the most alluring factors in their decision to join the course. This attraction to the course name "I Love Me" suggests that most of us are searching for ways to love ourselves more. I would even go as far as to say that low self-esteem exists in epidemic proportions, not only in the United States and Japan, but anywhere that I have worked in the world. As a human race we are looking for ways to accept and love ourselves more completely.

What is it that holds us back? The answer to this question can range from the philosophical to the mundane. When I have asked students to list on a sheet of paper five obstacles that limit or keep themselves from self-love, the responses that invariably show up are items related to prevailing *negative emotions or attitudes* or a lack of specific positive and *life-affirming habits.* When the students listed what they found difficult to accept in themselves, it usually had to do with qualities that they perceived as lacking in themselves.

Try this yourself. Take a few moments to list five obstacles to your own self-esteem. What is holding you back from loving yourself completely? Where do you feel that you are lacking? Even if you feel that you could fill an entire notebook with complaints or put-downs, let's start out with the five things that you find most deplorable or that seem to limit you from getting ahead.

1. _____
2. _____
3. _____
4. _____
5. _____

To be able to define something is the first step in finding a solution, so having done so we are already making progress. If you are just walking around with a vague sense that you don't like yourself, you are probably feeling depressed or frustrated most of the time. That little voice in your head is probably telling you where you are lacking and how unworthy you are, and what a failure you have turned out to be. There is nothing proactive in letting that self-talk rule your life. As you have learned with the Laws of the Mind, where we focus our attention is what we tend to perpetuate or bring about in our lives. Analizing your list you will find that virtually every item is something that can be changed once the proper attention is focused in that direction. Even if you have a fervent desire to have a better life experience, you need to be specific as to what that means to you in order to activate that genie in the bottle.

People who have high levels of self-esteem are people who take care of themselves. They do what is necessary to nurture their mind, body, and spirit in positive, proactive ways that enhance their life experience. Whether they drink eight glasses of water a day in order to flush their system of toxins and feel more physically present, or meditate to clear their minds of inconsequential debris, or devote an hour a day to reading and studying, they have acquired **life-affirming habits**. It is through these habits that they achieve their goals and allow the feelings of self-worth to grow day by day. In this section you will learn the *21-*

Day Secret, allowing you to become what you have most longed to be – a self-actualized individual who gets the most out of life. It starts, amazingly enough, with activating a system of positive habits.

Another characteristic of an individual with high self-esteem is the ability to neutralize **negative attitudes and emotions**. We are all instinctually capable of hate, resentment, prejudice, self-pity, guilt, envy and avarice, but we were not born with these traits. We've learned them through painful experiences that left impressions on our subconscious minds. Unless we take the responsibility to examine the source of that limiting programming, we will be compelled to act out on these impressions: This seriously limits our personal freedom.

A measure of self-esteem becomes even more self-esteem when we do what is necessary to take good care of ourselves. There are infinite levels of self-esteem, and each one raises our permission levels to possess a greater degree of connectedness to the Divine and a more satisfying life experience.

Let's look at a sample list from one of my students. These were five items that she listed as being obstacles to her fully loving herself:

> **I don't get enough exercise.**
> **I should be spending more time reading and studying.**
> **I have resentments towards my parents.**
> **I eat way too much junk food.**
> **I never seem to get anywhere on time.**

Okay, now let's break these down to find their source – which as I mentioned above, will invariably have something to do with a **negative habit** or lack of a positive **life-affirming** one, or a **negative attitude or emotion**.

I don't get enough exercise.

Exercise is certainly important for creating more muscle tone and balance, promoting better cardiovascular health, reducing stress and increasing energy. Yet, although we know these things, unless we create the **habit** of consistent exercise in our daily schedules, it tends to be something that we put off, knowing that our lives would improve find the self-discipline to work out on a regular basis. So, ...m on the list is a **lack of a positive habit**. We can go even deeper on this one. While exercise is indeed a behavior, not doing what is beneficial for us may have its origin in some kind of poor self image that can be linked to a program in our computer that inhibits taking affirmative action on our behalf. No matter how much you want to look and feel great, without establishing the habit in the subconscious mind, action will not be spontaneous and automatic. And without a positive self-image that supports life-affirming behavior, the desire to exercise will never find consistent expression in your outer world. The good news is that this can be accomplished in as little as 21 days!

I should be spending more time reading and studying.

Here's another example of a **lack of a positive habit**. It's a very good idea to read and study every day. This expands the mind, challenges you to think more and stretch your horizons, preparing you for a possible life or career change. By invoking your will power you may force yourself to read for 20 minutes or more a day. However, by communicating this to your subconscious mind, you can establish this daily practice in a way that becomes second nature to you and be able to concentrate better and retain more of what you read! Wouldn't that be easier than having to drag yourself by force of will?

I have resentments towards my parents.

Now, this is some of the deeper stuff – **negative emotions** that we can't seem to simply overcome by an act of will. We know that retaining these feelings are somehow hurting us but as much as we try to let them go, they keep surfacing and tend to rule our behavior. As you learned in an earlier chapter, these negative emotions are the result of painful or traumatic experiences in your childhood that formed perceptions of yourself, the world, and life in general. As long as these events and identifications remain trapped in your subconscious (which rules your behavior), you will continue to view yourself and others from a limited perspective. Wouldn't it be great to let go of such a heavy burden?

I eat way too much junk food.

Another deficiency on the **positive habit** board. If you are accustomed to eating what is fast and readily available, it's a matter of training your mind and body to crave those foods that are healthier and provide more enduring energy sources. You will tend to gravitate towards what you're used to eating, unless you change the habit within the subconscious mind. Are you starting to understand where I am going with all of this? All of our behavior comes from the subconscious mind. The subconscious performs exactly as it has been programmed to perform. Change the programming and the behavior follows suit.

I never seem to get anywhere on time.

This one's a piece of cake! We have an internal clock which can be programmed to wake us up at a specific time or to know automatically when a certain time frame has passed. This internal mechanism can even expand and contract time so that we can be more effective and flexible in our schedules. Through proper communication to the subconscious mind, you can program yourself to allow sufficient time to complete your tasks and be punctual. A side note here: If your lack of punctuality comes from a form of self-sabotage, in other words, not allowing yourself to do what it takes to be successful, then this could be related to **negative emotions or attitudes.**

This all boils down to the recurring theme of this book: if you want to change your life experience, you need to change the input in your computer. In this section you will learn how to lock in those life-affirming habits or get rid of the self-defeating ones and raise your self esteem levels. Then in the following section we'll get to the source of some of those negative emotions and attitudes. You are on your way to a much more effective usage of all that Random Access Memory (RAM) that is part of your God-given computer!

Getting into the habit

Anything that we have learned to do, such as brushing our teeth every morning and night, or looking both ways for traffic when we cross the street, is a result of habit formation. Our habits are formed in a ritualized pattern. Every experience we've had leaves its mark on the cerebral cortex of the brain. The cortex is the brain's "receiving station" for information sent to it by the nervous system. It is responsible for actually transforming that information into bodily action. Each time an experience is repeated, the mark, or imprint, is strengthened, making it even easier to repeat. Thoughts and behaviors become habitual through repetition.[29]

In that sense we are not much different than Pavlov's dogs who learned through repetition that the ringing of a bell was associated with mealtime. Ivan Pavlov, the Russian scientist, performed an experiment in the early part of the century. Every time he offered a meal to a group of dogs he would ring a bell. After a period of time all he would have to do was ring the bell and the dogs would start to salivate. This was the groundbreaking study that taught us about the conditioned reflex and basically paved the way to the behaviorist school of psychology.

Because so much of our behavior was programmed in early childhood, it's important to understand that we are pretty much responding to the "bell" in many of our actions. Something "rings" in our mind when we desire a snack or a cigarette and react on impulse with very little consciousness about what stimulates us to respond. Dr. M. Scott Peck in his wonderful book, *The Road Less Traveled,* makes a point about the difficulties we experience as adults when as children we never developed the ability to delay gratification. He describes this as a process of scheduling life's duties in such a way that we experience what is painful or less pleasurable first so that we can get it over with and then be fully present to enjoy the pleasure.[30] If we didn't learn this as children, we automatically seek out our pleasure first and for the most part those duties that require discipline or promote our self-mastery are put on the back burner.

When you make a New Year's resolution, you are attempting to create an action that is not compatible with your mind's current programming. You are exerting your force of will—a feature of the conscious mind. As you learned earlier in this book, the subconscious mind is seven to eight times stronger than the conscious mind, so within a short period of time the tendency is to fall back into the established behavioral patterns. This is why motivation rarely has a lasting effect. Without intervention the habits that are already programmed into the subconscious mind will invariably supersede the motivational material. If you want to change your actions, change your programming.

The 21-Day Secret

Have you ever heard the old adage "21 days to make a habit; 21 days to break a habit"? This saying is misleading. We assume that if we do or don't do something for 21 days – voila! A habit is created or broken. After all, many people have stopped smoking for at least three weeks and have started up again. And virtually everyone has gone on some kind of diet at some time in their lives where they changed their eating habits for a few weeks and eventually went right back to their old ways (and gained the weight back, too!)

By putting it to the test in several areas of my own life that needed improvement, I found that it's not what you *do* or *don't do* for 21 days: It's **how you represent it to yourself** during that period of time that either locks in the new habit or breaks the old. By "representing" I mean how it is communicated to your subconscious mind.

There is an amazing power in the number 21. Call it mystical if you'd like, but it does seem to be the prescribed number of days that the subconscious needs to receive the programming in order to bring about a permanent change.

Susumu Kameyama, founder of my Japanese promotion company, tried this out with great success. At 40, he got serious about taking care of his body. He joined a gym and started out with great enthusiasm, but was having difficulty staying consistent. He began to pay attention to his self-talk during this time and realized that he was virtually dragging himself to the gym, saying things to himself like "Oh, I can't stand this, but what choice do I have?" He started to use the positive messages and suggestions that I recommended, representing exercise to himself as something beneficial and pleasurable. By the 21st day, exercise had become an ingrained habit. Even when Susumu is traveling to exotic places like Peru, where there's not much access to a health club, he stays fit by taking long walks, working out in his room, or improvising some cardio-vascular activity. When Susumu returns to Japan, getting back to the gym takes no supreme effort on his part and he's amazed that all it took was changing the way that he represented it to himself.

You can use the *21-Day Secret* to lock in or break any habit in as little as three weeks, but the suggestions need to be given in the language of the subconscious, following the rules of suggestion. The best way to deliver the suggestion to the subconscious is in the *intentional state of hypnosis*, where there is direct access. Consistency here is the key. You must commit to 21 days without interruption, or begin the process all over again. You may notice an immediate change, but in order to lock in the habit, continue using the suggestion for the entire three weeks. This will make the new behavior *second nature to you*, meaning that even if you have lapses, you can easily pick up where you left off.

Start Out Slowly

You really can change habits in 21 days, but instead of starting with the major issues, I strongly recommend that you start out slowly. For instance, if you smoke, there's some that would say that smoking is a habit. Others claim it's an addiction. Perhaps it's a bit of both. People who smoke often have deeper issues that are being covered up by the habit. This is called *mood-altering behavior.* The smoking appears to help the individual repress uncomfortable emotions buried in the subconscious. Or, it could be a way of dealing with stress. For this reason, it's not a good idea to begin working on the smoking until you can get to the deeper issues. If you smoke, you may want to start out with eliminating stress. Stress is a learned behavior and can be modified through hypnosis. As you relax more and are able to deal effectively with the challenges of daily life, you will progress to a point that giving up smoking will seem natural to you. At that point, use the *21-Day Secret* to knock it out for once and for all! If you were to attempt to make quitting smoking your first goal without first examining and eliminating the core issues around this habit, you may be setting yourself up for failure.

Do you remember the story of Hercules? He was given seemingly impossible tasks to prove his worthiness as a warrior. One of them required that he slay the Hydra – a monster with a hundred heads. As he proceeded to chop off the heads with his sword, a new head would instantly pop up in its place. The only way he could finally kill the Hydra, was by stabbing its heart. He had to get to the core.

You will eventually get rid of all your bad habits by faithfully using these techniques. You can even banish negative emotions and attitudes that have been holding you back from expressing your full potential, however, you must first get to the core issues.

Weight control is another example of starting out too ambitiously. While we obviously gain weight from over-eating and indulging in the wrong foods, being overweight often has to do with core issues of self-esteem. If you do not have a self-image that supports your looking and feeling good, all the diets in the world will eventually fail. You may lose weight for a time, but then, the inevitable yo-yo syndrome puts it right back on.

By starting slowly, I mean that you should choose a simple habit, such as drinking eight glasses of water a day, or getting up at a certain time on weekdays. There is a whole list below of ideas to get you started. These examples may not be your first priority, but they will make a tremendous difference to your sense of self-worth. A friend shared with me recently that just by getting into the habit of flossing she was noticing a lot of positive changes going on in her life. What happens in these cases is that change becomes exponential: small changes lead to big changes. When you create a life-affirming habit, as trivial as it may seem, this new habit opens the door for new and better habits. Success begets more success. And pretty soon you can conquer those major issues with very little resistance.

Levanah Shel B'dolak, a respected teacher and healer, has a wonderful concept that she calls "raising your permission levels." Many people are not aware that they have limiting beliefs and self-images that make their goals seem unreachable. It's almost as if we have to give ourselves permission on an inner level in order to make our dreams come true. For instance, you may long to be self-employed and not have to deal with small-minded and controlling managers. Yet if you do not create a vision of yourself that permits you to not be dependent on a fixed salary, you would either never take the risk of going out on your own, or set yourself up for failure. What I have found in my own experience is that the more beneficial habits I have created through the *21-Day Secret*, the more permission I am giving myself to live fully, joyfully, and freely.

In seminars, I ask participants to fill in the blank and choose the appropriate ending for one of the following sentences. This starts the process of choosing the habit(s) to launch their first 21-day cycle. To begin your own 21-day program, choose the sentence (a,b,or c) with the word that most closely describes what you want to accomplish, and then fill in the blank.

a) By acquiring the habit of _____, my life is becoming happier.

b) By acquiring the habit of _____, my life is becoming more successful.

c) By acquiring the habit of _____, my life is becoming more abundant.

Here are some possible habits that you might like to change or lock onto to get you started:

- **Drinking 8-10 glasses of water per day.**
- **Waking up at _____ effortlessly _____days per week.**
- **Eating more fruits and vegetable.**
- **Meditating for _____ minutes every day.**
- **Reading for _____ minutes _____times per week.**
- **Walking (or another safe form of exercise) for _____ minutes _____ days per week.**
- **Listening more carefully and pausing before you respond.**
- **Scheduling more time with your family members.**
- **Keeping a diary or journal.**
- **Flossing your teeth.**

• Practice stretching each morning or night.

• Deep breathing and relaxation.

• Arriving punctually to appointments.

• Smiling or laughing more often.

• Filing and/or organizing your paper work.

• Hanging up your clothes or putting them away immediately.

Rules of Suggestion

By the word "suggestion" we mean any word, group of words, phrases, idea or group of ideas that are presented to the subconscious in its particular vernacular for the purpose of bringing about a reorganization of thoughts and actions. A suggestion can be given in the form of a script designed around a certain theme, such as instilling a healthy lifestyle. You can combine themes providing that they are compatible, such as drinking water, diet and exercise. But if you were to add organizing your paperwork and saving money, you would be overloading the subconscious, and thus, defeating the purpose. Don't expect to change every negative detail of your life in your first 21-day cycle! You would only be setting yourself up to fail.

The length of the script can be from a few paragraphs long to several pages. The ideal length is roughly one hand-written page long. When you are preparing a suggestion I recommend that you first make a worksheet, outlining what behavior, attitude, or emotion you want to change in your life, and how your current behavior, attitude, or emotion manifests in a negative way. Unfortunately, it is much easier for us to find ways to put ourselves down than to build ourselves up. Then, on a separate piece of paper begin to write a suggestion for each of the items, adhering to the rules of suggestion you will find in this chapter.

There are many tapes and books available containing standardized scripts for any number of habits, attitudes, and emotions that you may like to change. While you may want to refer to them to get some ideas, I have found that the personalized suggestion is the best way to go. I know that human nature always looks for the easiest way, but if you really want to get to the root of some negative programming, the suggestions must be personalized. Not everyone has the same reasons for being overweight, procrastinating, or smoking, and no standardized script can address all of those reasons. By simply applying someone else's suggestion, this will only give the Band-Aid effect – covering up something that reaches in much deeper into your psyche. The more willing you are to explore the sources of your self-sabotaging behavior, the more you are able to yank them out by the roots and no longer be bound by the compulsions.

I have provided two sample worksheets and scripts to give you an idea of how to write your personalized suggestion. Feel free to use any phrases that work for you, but make sure that you create a suggestion for every item on your worksheet. Adhering to the rules of suggestion in your final draft guarantees much greater results, but don't worry about making mistakes. The most important element at play here is your *intent*. This activates the *Law of Concentrated Attention*, letting your subconscious know that you are ready for a change and directing it on how to bring about that change. Even taking the time to break down the negative behavior into components is a very positive step, as you are being proactive rather than giving into the usual frustrations.

Getting Started

STEP ONE: Choose a habit, attitude or emotion that you'd like to change. Or, think of some positive behavior that you'd like to have as part of your daily routine.

STEP TWO: Prepare a worksheet. In Column A write down what you want to change in your life. Remember to work on a single theme or combine similar ones. In Column B write down how the negative behavior currently manifests in your life. Refer to the two sample worksheets below to see how this is done.

Sample Worksheet I – Creating a Healthy Lifestyle

(A)

1. I want to change my sedentary lifestyle.

(B)

1. Hardly do any exercise
2. Mostly inactive

	3. Lacking energy and motivation
2. I want to change my appearance.	1. Excess body fat
	2. Wearing larger clothing sizes
	3. Feel bad about myself
3. I want to change my poor eating habits.	1. Eat too much fat and sweets
	2. Not enough vegetables
	3. Inconsistent about my eating schedule

Sample Worksheet II – Overcoming Procrastination

(A)	(B)
1. I want to change my habit of putting things off until the last minute	1. I waste a lot of time
	2. Don't feel good about myself
	3. I'm not activating my full potential
	4. I get stressed out trying to catch up
2. I want to have my paperwork more organized	1. I can't ever find what I need
	2. I get frustrated over lack of order
	3. I don't accomplish much
	4. More stuff is piling up

As you can see, both of these worksheets describe in detail what the individual wants to modify according to his or her own subjective needs. The art of suggestion-writing is to take every negative and turn it into a positive. Although this is not the way we are used to communicating to ourselves, it is the only effective way to get the subconscious to cooperate in effecting a permanent change. Following the Rules of Suggestion you will find a script for both of these worksheets.

STEP THREE: Review the seven Rules of Suggestion outlined below. This is the language structure of your subconscious mind. By adhering to these rules as much as possible when creating your own script, you will get definite results!

RULE #1: Be Positive

Whenever possible stay away from negative words such as **try, don't, maybe, pain, can't, failure**, etc. These words carry an emotional charge

89

and can activate the *Law of Dominant Effect,* drawing away energy from your goal and focusing it on negative past patterns. In your suggestion describe what you want to experience. Don't talk about what you want to move away from, talk about what you want to move towards. Don't talk about what you want to get out of your life. Talk about what you want to bring into your life.

Incorrect Example I: I am trying to get out of the habit of sitting and watching television night after night. What you are doing here is emphasizing the negative pattern. Also the use of the word *try* will activate the Law of Reversed Effect.

Correct Example I: Every night gives me an opportunity to work on my body. Whether stretching, doing resistance training, or cardiovascular activity, I am taking advantage of every opportunity to exercise.

Incorrect Example II: I don't want to keep feeling bad about putting things off – it's time to change. No need to put yourself down—it's counterproductive. Remember, suggestion is a much different way of communicating with yourself than you are used to.

Correct Example II: I accomplish all of my tasks in a timely manner. This may actually feel like you are "fibbing" to yourself, and that's perfectly okay, at least for suggestion-creating purposes. You must directly motivate the subconscious to bring about the change.

RULE #2: Use the Present Tense

The subconscious is existential, which means that it only exists in the present. Through hypnosis a subject can be taken back to a moment in the past that is relived as if it were happening at this very moment. The future is not real to the subconscious, this is why when we make comments such as "When x,y,z happens I will be happy" we are literally postponing our happiness. The subconscious only knows what is happening now, so formulate your suggestions in the present tense, such as "I am happy". Avoid the word "will".

Incorrect Example I: I will make exercising a part of my daily routine. Here the subconscious knows perfectly well that there is no exercising going on *now.* The word "will" has no real meaning to the subconscious mind.

Correct Example I: **Exercise is a part of my daily routine.** Again, it may seem odd to you to be telling yourself something that you may not be doing, but this is how to represent correctly to your subconscious.

Incorrect Example II: **I plan on getting my papers organized this year.** This is far too abstract for your subconscious, which needs to be directed as if it were a child.

Correct Example II: **I consistently organize my paperwork, filing away all documents as soon as they cross my desk.**

There are two exceptions to Rule #2:

1) Suggestions for healing an injured body part should be taken in steps. For example, in the case of an ulcer, saying "My stomach feels great" is inappropriate because the subconscious is in charge of the functioning of the organs and is aware that there is a problem. In this case, it is better to say, "Every day my stomach is getting stronger and healthier."

2) If you are rehearsing for a future event, such as a test, instead of saying "I feel so confident when I take my test" you can actually specify the date. For example, *"On January 20 I am sitting in the classroom taking a deep cleansing breath as I prepare for my exam. I have tremendous confidence as I stretch my fingers and pick up my pen. All of the information flows freely because I know that I am prepared."*

* It is also important to not refer to past negative experience; for instance: *"From now on I'm not going to let my negative self-image get in the way of my working out."* This will tend to lock in the negative habit. The correct presentation would be: *"From this day forward I take full responsibility for my self-image. Nothing that has happened can effect the positive feelings that I am developing day by day. Working out enhances my growing self-love."*

RULE #3: Be Specific And Detailed

Suggestion scripts are more effective when you isolate an area of your life that needs change and then stick to that subject for the 21 days. You can combine similar suggestions such as those in the example where we have exercise, appearance and eating habits linked. But if you are going to work on exercise, relationship difficulties, and organizing your paperwork, you are not giving the adequate amount of specific focus. Remember the *Law of Concentrated Attention* and design your suggestions so that they aim directly at their target.

In the (B) column of the worksheet you should be very specific when you list all the ways that your negative habits are manifesting. Then, on the final draft, it will be quite easy to turn each one around as you familiarize yourself with the Rules of Suggestion.

You may notice some changes occurring almost immediately, but I feel that it's important to continue to use the suggestion for a minimum of 21 days in order to lock in the new behavioral pattern.

Incorrect Example I : Exercising is fun. I welcome it into my life. This works well as an affirmation that you can repeat to yourself throughout the day. However, you need to be more descriptive in the actual suggestion.

Correct Example I: I enjoy exercising. I welcome the feeling of exhilaration that comes after a good workout. I know that I am challenging myself to achieve my personal best and even when I question if I can go on, I am easily getting that additional spurt of energy to carry me through another productive workout. Notice here how much the subconscious is being stimulated to respond to the emotional impact of the suggestion.

Incorrect Example II: I am organizing every aspect of my life. This is another great affirmation, but in terms of suggestion, it needs to be much more specific. The subconscious needs a literal explanation of what to organize.

Correct Example II: How wonderful it feels to have every aspect of my life organized: My paperwork is up to date; my bills are being paid on time; and I am on track with all of my projects. I have much more guilt-free spare time to enjoy myself now. This works hand in hand with the *Law of Dominant Effect*: the subconscious is the imaginative and emotional part of your mind.

RULE #4: Avoid Perfectionism!

When you make suggestions that require you to be perfect or the best at something, you are falling into a trap of someone else's projection of what perfect may be: This could be your parents, the media, a teacher from the past, a critical spouse or boss. This is another set up for failure, because the *Law of Dominant Effect* will shift the energy to the prevalent emotional tone of "not being good enough". I am aware that many athletes, models and actors may have built up very attractive bodies by using these types of suggestions, but they are not necessarily good for overall mental health. Perfectionism, in any area of life is a myth. We are human and therefore, subject to weakness and failures. Even if you are doing an ultimate job in one or more areas of your life, think about the price you may be paying by being unbalanced in other realms. The moment you find yourself using a suggestion that says that you have to be the best, make sure to question if that message is coming from *your spirit* or from some programming of the consensus reality.

The one exception here is when you are using self-hypnosis to improve your sports performance, such as a better tennis or golf swing. While it is okay to suggest being the best for purposes of competition, avoid the word "perfect". And make sure to always leave room for being satisfied with each level of improvement.

Incorrect Example I: I am achieving the perfect body. No such thing! There's always someone out there that you will wind up comparing yourself unfavorably to.

Correct Example I: I am working toward my personal best and loving myself every step of the way.

Incorrect Example II: I feel more accepted because I am more productive. The foundation of "SELF" is lacking here. We shouldn't make changes just to please others.

Correct Example II: My self-esteem is growing because I make better use of my time. I feel like a winner!

RULE #5: Be Repetitive

Habits were formed by repeated behavioral patterns. We can change, modify or replace a habit in much less time than it took to form one, but repetition is the key to successfully implanting new suggestions. Feel free to repeat the same phrase over and over again in your suggestion or use positive messaging as many times a day as you'd like, such as, **"I enjoy peace of mind as I accomplish my tasks"**. This way, the imprint is strengthened on the cerebral cortex of the brain.

RULE #6: Talk About Action, Not Ability

Be wary of talking about what you "can" do or what you'd "like" to accomplish. This becomes lip service, because the subconscious is activated mainly by direct commands.

<u>Incorrect Example I</u>: **I know I can get my body in shape. I feel that I can accomplish great things with this body.** Referring to ability rather than action will not be sufficient in stimulating the subconscious mind into action.

<u>Correct Example I</u>: **My body is getting into shape. Day by day tremendous changes are occurring in all the muscles groups of my body. I am burning fat and converting it into lean muscle mass.**

<u>Incorrect Example II</u>: **Taking care of my work on a timely basis is a way that my potential can be realized.** This is a truism, but useless as a suggestion. The subconscious has to be told what to do.

<u>Correct Example II</u>: **Each day I measure my time in order to activate my full potential. I am motivated to complete the work at hand as this allows me to fully enjoy my free time. I am a winner!**

RULE #7: Be Creative and Imaginative!

Imagination and emotion dominate the subconscious mind. In order to swing the primary focus of energy to your goal (*Law of Dominant Effect*), strive to inspire and animate your subconscious by using very emotionally charged superlatives such as **energetic, exhilarating, extraordinary, sensational, tremendous, exceptional, delightful, thrilling, etc.** It is perfectly okay to exaggerate, except in the case of healing an organ or seeking perfectionism.

By keeping these seven rules in mind, formulating suggestion becomes spontaneous and effective; subsequently, we find that we are much more aware of those typical daily put-down phrases that can become self-fulfilling prophecies. When you catch yourself saying something negative or something that is working against you, just say "Cancel", repair it and move on.

STEP FOUR: Now it's time to write a script. Take those negatives and turn them into positives. Don't worry if it doesn't seem as polished as the examples below. With practice you will develop a more refined technique, just as if you were learning how to play an instrument or draw. THE VITAL POINT IS THAT YOU ARE TELLING YOUR SUBCONSCIOUS WHAT YOU DESIRE! Re-read your script several times to make sure that you have not inadvertently put in any negative phrases or verbs in the future tense, such as **try**, **maybe**, **can**, or **will**.

Below are the finished products from both of the worksheets in Step Two. All of the negative statements have been converted to positive ones, adhering to the rules of suggestion.

Sample Script: Creating a Healthy Lifestyle

Exercise is becoming a part of my lifestyle. I embrace this new way of living because I love the way I feel, I love the way I look, and I love the way my body is becoming more flexible and healthy. I am open to a variety of different exercises because I enjoy trying new things and finding new ways to move my body. I am easily fitting the appropriate number of workouts into my lifestyle. I have time now to devote to my self-improvement and I feel much more energetic and motivated to keep growing and learning.

All of this increased activity is melting away excess body fat and I am becoming leaner and trimmer. I find my clothes getting loose and I am happily anticipating fitting into my favorite dresses and also buying new clothes to show off my attractive figure. I feel so good about myself because I am taking action toward creating this fabulous new me.

I nourish myself to provide adequate energy for my workouts. I enjoy taking responsibility for the food that I eat, knowing that I am supplying my body with proper fuel and nutrition. I am balanced in the way that I eat so that I get the most energy out of my food. Vegetables are plentiful in my diet. I am so excited about the variety that are available and I am learning new ways to prepare them in a cornucopia of delights. I am satisfied with my meals because I am accountable for my energy levels. I am constantly aware of what my body needs and when. Fats and sugars are rapidly forming less and less of my daily food intake, yet I allow myself treats from time to time to reward myself for my wonderful changes.

All of the words, ideas and phrases contained within this suggestion are creating a positive impact upon my subconscious mind. All of the words, ideas and phrases are becoming reality in my life.

Sample Script: Overcoming Procrastination

How wonderful it feels to be current with all my work. I use my time in a measured way, so that at the end of the day, I feel good about what I have accomplished. Getting projects done in a timely manner is activating my full potential and I feel so much better about myself. I am so relaxed now that I complete my work with plenty of spare time. This provides me with lots of time to do the things I like to do. I am finishing my projects way ahead of schedule. I feel like a winner. There's no limit to what I can accomplish.

As new paperwork and mail cross my desk, I take the necessary moments to deal with them and dispose of them as required. My desk is so much more organized and this causes my thoughts to be more organized. With my thoughts in order I am accomplishing more than ever before. Because my work is taken care of in a timely manner, it is easy to have all the pertinent information on hand. My life is uncomplicated with everything so organized. I feel so good and relaxed. I feel like a winner.

All of the words, ideas and phrases contained within this suggestion are creating a positive impact upon my subconscious mind. All of the words, ideas and phrases are becoming reality in my life.

STEP FIVE: Find a key word or a key phrase that embodies the emotional tone of your suggestion. For instance, if you are working on stress control, you might like the imagery of "a tranquil ocean", or the feeling of "peace and harmony". The key phrase should not refer to the negative behavior. For instance, in Example I, "Creating a Healthy Lifestyle" works perfectly well for a key phrase. A more simplified version may be "Healthy Life".

In the second example, "Overcoming Procrastination" as a key phrase would not be acceptable, as it only emphasizes the negative behavior. Some effective choices would be "Time is my friend" or "Winning".

The key word or key phrase is subjective. It can even be a symbol or an image associated with your goal; however, it should have special meaning for you as it will be used as a post-hypnotic suggestion throughout the day to motivate and relax you, or any time you notice yourself in an unintentional state of hypnosis.

The Next Step

Now you have a finished product with a key word or phrase. You can deliver the suggestion to your subconscious in several ways. Experiment with them to find out which works best for you. In order to bypass the critical factor of the mind, you should first do some kind of relaxation ritual in order to create a state of intentional hypnosis. This will ensure that the subconscious is in the dominant position and open to suggestion. There are several excellent induction methods included in this *Tool Kit* as well as in the *Troubleshooting* section.

Whenever possible, you should practice some form of progressive relaxation in order to rid your body and mind of the natural stressors that accumulate as part of daily life. Then you will have sufficient receptivity for effectively delivering the suggestion. If you are ever short on time you can bypass the induction process once you have implanted a post-hypnotic cue. (See "Effective Inductions" and "Post-Hypnotics"). This allows you to re-enter a comfortable level of trance within moments and be ready to receive the programming.

Any of the following options you choose should be used consistently for a 21-day period to ensure the full participation of the subconscious mind.

MEMORIZING THE SCRIPT: Once you enter trance you simply run through the script in your mind. By ending your script with the following words, it serves as a direct order to your subconscious to carry out all of the suggestions to the letter: *"All of the words, ideas and phrases contained within this suggestion are creating a positive impact upon my subconscious mind. All of the words, ideas and phrases are becoming reality in my life."* Memorizing the script, however, is probably the least desirable technique since you are relying on memory and you will more than likely keep the conscious mind too present. Considering the ultra-selective nature of the conscious mind this may defeat the purpose. Individuals who memorize easily can use this method with good results.

PRE-RECORDING A TAPE: Either record the tape in your own voice or have someone do it for you. **Make sure to review the instructions for preparing your own cassettes in the beginning of this section before you begin.** The first part of the tape should be your favorite induction/progressive relaxation technique. Next read your suggestion into the microphone three times. Be sure to include the phrase, *"All of the words, ideas and phrases contained within this suggestion are creating a positive impact upon my subconscious mind. All of the words, ideas and phrases are becoming reality in my life"*. End the tape with an "awakening" procedure. For example, "as I count now from one to five, I come back to full awareness, feeling calm, refreshed and relaxed. 1-2-3-4-5. Eyes open. Wide awake.

USE A KEY WORD OR PHRASE: This innovative method comes from the late Charles Tebbets' *Self Hypnosis and Other Mind Expanding Techniques.* My personal favorite, it makes use of code, symbol, word or phrase which "plays back" the suggestion to the subconscious mind in a virtually effortless manner. Before getting ready to enter trance, read your suggestion out loud, slowly, three times. If you are not in a place that you can do this privately, read it to yourself four or five times. Always end with these words *"all of the ideas, words and phrases contained within this suggestion are symbolized by the key word/phrase _____"*, filling in the blank with your chosen key word or phrase. Get into a comfortable position and practice your induction or use your post-hypnotic cue to enter trance. Then simply repeat mentally your key word, phrase or object, or visualize the object that represents your goal. The suggestions that you read out loud only moments before will be fed directly into your subconscious. You should remain in this phase for at least seven minutes and then make sure to mentally count yourself out of trance before opening your eyes.

The Power of Ritual

Your suggestion should be implanted in the subconscious mind consistently for 21 days in whatever format you choose. Although the hypnotic state greatly facilitates its acceptance, you can also use the script as a prayer. The more you learn how to activate the *Law of Concentrated Attention*, the quicker you will be able to manifest amazing things in your life.

Practicing your suggestion daily at about the same time can intensify the ritual of the 21 days. Try having a special area set up and perhaps even light a candle for the duration of the session. Anything that you can do to add to the build up of concentrated attention will focus that laser beam right on your goal and make it a reality. Make sure to visualize or imagine your goal or end result as you practice your self-hypnosis. As you read on in this section you will find out how to magnify your results by adding visualization and imagery formulas designed to your particular mode of perception.

A word of caution here: While your suggestions might involve others in your world (such as improving communication with your family members or having a more harmonious work environment) you should never create and use a suggestion that influences the habits or behaviors of any one else. For example, although you might be convinced that if your teenage son spent more time studying, it would greatly improve his grade point average, he is the one who has to make that decision and do the 21-day ritual. You can help him with writing his suggestion, but you cannot do your own ritual based around changing his behavior. This is a violation of free will. No matter how pure your intentions may be to help your loved ones, you must respect the fact that human beings have the divine right of choice. Creating a suggestion in which you develop more tolerance and patience with your loved ones is an acceptable alternative.

Guided Imagery

Every person receives and processes information from the external world through the doorways of the five senses. Three of the senses, namely: sight, hearing, and feeling, are greater equipped to act as filters and process incoming data. These are called the Learning Channels. This information is then recorded onto our brains as sensory imprints, which are later translated into thoughts, words and action channeled through our personal map of reality.

Generally, one of these three learning channels is more developed than the other two. It is through this channel that the individual learns and makes distinctions. The dominant sense or channel is referred to as our primary representational system and individuals are referred to as being VISUAL, AUDITORY, OR KINESTHETIC. You may not be familiar with this terminology—it comes from the technology of NLP (Neuro-Linguistic Programming) which was founded by John Grinder and Richard Bandler. NLP breaks down learning and perception into their basic components in order to streamline the communication process.

Take the self-test on page 106 to determine which learning channel is most significant in creating your particular map of reality.

I have chosen to use the term "Guided Imagery" rather than "Visualization" in this manual in recognition that not all of us can easily "see" an image on our mental screen. This might come rather easily to a Visual type, but the Auditory or Kinesthetic might not have that inner sense as well developed. A way that you can flex all of your sensory muscles is to work with the following list of different sensory images. Each category will challenge you to awaken that particular sense. Practice daily until it becomes effortless to imagine. You can also make your own lists and have someone read them out loud to you or record them on tape. The more you can develop your inner vision, the more magnetic attraction your thoughts create.

I have also achieved significant results from using directed imagery while performing physical exercise. This is due to the vital connection being made between the mind and the body. Through a study with a personal trainer, we found that not only were results enhanced from using the imagery, it also made exercising less tedious, even fun! One of my favorite scenarios—being primarily a Visual—helped me burn excess body fat. I would visualize the Wicked Witch of the West from the Wizard of Oz melting away into the floor while thinking the phrase "I'm shrinking, I'm melting".

The self-test is not meant to pinpoint precisely your representational system, but it can be valuable in letting you know how your neurotransmitters carry information to the cells of the body. Below is a brief explanation of how each of the representational systems process information and communicate verbally and non-verbally. Because the way we communicate reflects our own personal map of reality it is often prone to distortions and misunderstanding. You might be interested in studying more about this in order to communicate better with members of your family and co-workers who may process through a different channel. One of the best books on the subject is *Influencing with Integrity* by Genie LaBorde.

Visual

"Can you see what I'm getting at?"
"Just explain it to me in black and white."
"Do you get the picture?"

These are expressions that Visuals often use. This individual processes information primarily through sight, capturing and learning everything as if through the lens of a camera. These types store information in their memory banks in photographic form and when remembering something will search their memory files to find a mental image. Predicates and descriptive words used will describe colors, sizes, shapes and shades. The Visual learns best from reading, observing, and examining graphic representations. To effectively communicate with a Visual you must enter their world and try to see through their eyes. You may identify a Visual from body movements (generally still), voice speed (speaks rapidly) and eye movements (eyes defocused straight ahead as if looking for the answer somewhere in the brain; or looking up to the corner of either eye). Words that are most appealing to the Visual include the following: *see, look, watch, focus, clear, foggy, picture, reveal, notice, appear, perspective, visualize* and *illustrate.*

Auditory

"That sounds strange to me."
"Listen to what I'm trying to tell you."
"That really rings a bell."

These are expressions that an Auditory often uses. This individual processes information through the ears, capturing and learning everything as if recorded on tape. These types store information in their memory banks as sounds and voices and when remembering something will rewind the tape and hear how it sounded. Predicates and descriptive words used describe sounds, levels, timbre, noises and rhythms. The Auditory learns best from listening, both to others and to their internal dialogue. To effectively communicate with an Auditory you must enter their world and try to hear through their ears. You may identify an Auditory from body movements (rhythmic like a metronome), and eye movements (side to side at ear level) or moving their head in the direction of the sound. Words that are most appealing to the Auditory include the following: *listen, said, hear, sounds like, speak, rhyme, accent, amplify, voice* and *tune.*

Kinesthetic

"That hits me right in my gut."
"That doesn't sit well with me."
"What you're telling me moves me deeply."

These are the expressions that a Kinesthetic often uses. This individual processes information through the feelings, capturing and learning everything like a radar or emotional antenna. These types store information in their memory bank as sensations and when remembering something will go back to how they felt at that moment. Predicates and descriptive words used will describe emotions, sensations, textures, and interpretations as they learn more by experiencing. You may identify a Kinesthetic by body movements (actively shifting around), voice speed (rather slow), and eye movements (looking down to their dominant hand side). Words that are most appealing to the Kinesthetic include the following: *grasp, touch, feel, hold it, contact, smooth, impact,* and *handle.*

What is Your Representational Preference?

Although you use all of the representational systems to process information, this self-test will help you determine your bias. Once you are aware of your preference you may decide to incorporate similar guided imagery in order to enhance the power of your suggestion. For instance, if you are a Visual type and you are working on getting more physically fit, *see* yourself wearing the types of clothes that you would like to wear or get a distinct vision of the muscle definition that you are creating. If you are an Auditory type working on manifesting more income, *hear* the comments that your friends and family members are making about your success. If you are a Kinesthetic type working on becoming more organized, *feel* the sense of satisfaction that comes from having your paperwork filed and easily accessible.

Circle the FIRST response that you relate to in each question. When finished, total the A's, B's, and C's separately. Where you see the highest score will likely represent the sense that you prefer for storing information in your brain as well as your communication style. You will usually find that one letter outscores the other, with another one close by. The third letter would be the weakest or least used representation system. It is also not unusual to find the scores evenly distributed among the three letters.

Representational System—Self Test

1. When you relate wonderfully with someone you just meet, you experience
   A. being with a person who sees things from your point of view.
   B. having the opportunity to talk to someone who communicates as you do.
   C. sharing comfortably your feelings with another person.

2. The way you memorize names or telephone numbers is
   A. using visual images or writing down and mentally photographing them.
   B. repeating out loud or using rhyming words to remember.
   C. writing it down several times or by touch on the telephone pad.

3. On an outing to the beach, what most attracts you is
   A. the blue-green water, the clouds in the sky, the formations in the sand.
   B. the sound of the surf crashing on the sand and the sea gulls calling out.
   C. the feel of the breezes and sun, the sand under your feet, the water on your toes.

4. You tend to communicate what is going on with you by
   A. the way you dress.
   B. the tone of your voice.
   C. sharing the way you feel.

5. When you decorate a room you strive to
   A. choose colors and styles that are most pleasing to the eye.
   B. decorate with what most resonates with you, using harmonious forms and colors.
   C. create a cozy niche which feels comfortable to you.

6. While listening to music, what is your INNER reaction?
   A. Flights of imagination.
   B. Getting into the tone, rhythm, and lyrics.
   C. Experiencing a pleasant vibration in your body, wanting to move with the music.

7. When you go to a movie, you are MOST affected by
   A. the color, the action, the cinematography, the location.
   B. the dialogue, the background sounds and music.
   C. your emotional responses (i.e. suspense, sadness, joy).

8. When installing a difficult new program in your computer you are likely to
   A. read the instructions and follow them step-by-step.
   B. call technical support so that they can guide you through it.
   C. have someone there to walk you through the set-up if possible.

9. When you are filled with well being, your relationship to the outer world is
   A. perceiving all as bright and full of light.
   B. in tune, experiencing a sense of harmony.
   C. feeling very energized and alive.

10. An associate made a proposal that you are not in agreement with. The response you most identify with is:
   A. I don't agree with your point of view.
   B. That doesn't sound right to me.
   C. It just doesn't feel right to me.

11. What turns you on most in sex is
   A. being aware of all of the movement and action.
   B. hearing the sounds and words that are spoken.
   C. feeling all of the sensations.

12. When you fall in love, the first thing that you are aware of is
   A. how wonderful your lover looks to you.
   B. your reaction to the way your lover talks, or something they said.
   C. a special way that this person makes you feel.

13. When traveling to new places, the FIRST thing you notice is
   A. how the place looks.
   B. the different sounds that are associated with it.
   C. the new feelings that surround it.

14. When driving in a new city and lost, you would
   A. buy a map and guide yourself there.
   B. stop at a service station to get directions.
   C. drive around to get a sense of direction - then see if you can find your way.

15. Some of your favorite activities are
   A. reading, movies, art galleries, traveling to lovely scenery.
   B. listening to music, hearing the news, concerts, being at the ocean at night, talking.
   C. dancing, physical activities, hobbies, cooking, making things.

16. In order to sleep comfortably at night, what's most important to you is
   A. the room needs to be darkened just right.
   B. the room is quiet with muted background noises.
   C. the bed and weight of the covers feels just right.

Now total the number of each letter you have chosen and list it below to see your representational preference.

*A*_____   *B*_____   *C*_____
    VISUAL   *AUDITORY*   *KINESTHETIC*

Magnify Your Inner Vision
Exercise

When you add the ingredient of guided imagery to your suggestions you intensify the focus of the laser beam, bringing your goals into manifestation much more rapidly. How clearly can you see, hear, smell, feel and taste on your mental screen? Have someone read the list below and determine which of your inner senses are strong and which ones need more practice. Don't be concerned if you show weakness in some of these areas. Your inner senses are like muscles that have become atrophied from lack of use and can surely be built up by doing these exercises consistently. You will be amazed at how skillful you become at visualizing and imagining your goals!

VISUAL IMAGES: Take note of how clearly and detailed each one appears on your mental screen.

A tiger
A clown
Your mother's face
A rose
President Clinton
A cathedral or temple
Your living room
The full moon

VISUAL MOVEMENT IMAGES: These images are in motion. Can you capture them?

A kitten lapping milk from a bowl
A waterfall
A kite flying in the breeze
Your best friend walking towards you
An airplane taking off

AUDITORY IMAGES: Sounds

Chimes blowing in the wind
Young children giggling
A drum solo
An alarm clock going off

OLFACTORY IMAGES: Smells

Burning leaves
Gardenia blossoms
Sea air
Your favorite meal being prepared

GUSTATORY IMAGES: Tastes

Lemon juice
Chili peppers
Toothpaste
Chocolate ice cream

SENSORY IMAGES: Textures and Touch

Stroking a cat's fur
Diving or jumping into a swimming pool on a warm day
Being wrapped in a warm blanket
Holding hands with a loved one

KINESTHETIC IMAGES: Physical sensations and movements

How you feel when you run
Being hugged
Being chilly
Carrying something heavy

So, how did you do? Make sure to record your results below. You can practice with these same images or invent some of your own.

Strongest Images: _____

_____

Weakest Images: _____

_____

Affirmations and Positive Messaging

Affirmations are defined as statements that refer to universal truths and are timeless in nature, such as *Love, health and abundance are my birthright* or *Universal wisdom is guiding me in all of my actions.* Gawain, in her landmark book *Creative Visualization,* explains how powerful these statements can be in creating our reality.[31] I agree that affirmations are really quite beautiful and spiritual, but they tend to be general rather than specific. For this reason, unless they are personally structured, they tend to create more of a Band-Aid effect rather than penetrating down to the deeper core issues which block us from acquiring positive action towards our goals. For more on this, go back and re-read the section on "The First Thought" in *Power Supply.*

The aim of positive messaging is to counteract those times when we spontaneously enter into *unintentional states of hypnosis* and automatically accept or dispatch detrimental programming that stimulates the subconscious or the body part into action. As you become aware of your self-talk during those lull periods, such as driving your car or washing your dishes, begin to replace the old tapes (such as "Today isn't my day" or "No one seems to care about me") with an affirmation or a positive message. Even if you stop the negative statement by declaring "Cancel", you are making great strides in taking control of your own mind.

Try some of the affirmations listed below or experiment with building some positive messages to interject into your quiet moments throughout the day. According to Stephen Covey, author of *The 7 Habits of Highly Effective People,* "a good affirmation has five basic ingredients: it's *personal*, it's *positive*, it's *present tense*, it's *visual*, and it's *emotional*",[32] so it is structured very much like suggestion.

When worded according to the rules of suggestion, positive messages have the capacity to reach into our old belief structures, and shape a new perspective that supports our positive intentions. Through the rule of repetition, amazing changes can occur from these worthwhile statements. Visualizing or imagining the realization of your goals adds tremendous power to your affirmations and positive messages. To affirm is to create. That which we affirm becomes our reality.

- **Every day in every way, I am getting better and better and better.**
- **I am an enlightened being, full of light and love.**
- **I am the master of my own life, architect of my destiny.**
- **I have unchangeable faith in myself.**
- **I find all answers and wisdom within me.**
- **I love myself and accept myself as I am.**
- **My relationship with _____ is becoming fuller and happier each day.**
- **Abundance is my natural state. I accept it fully now.**
- **_____ comes effortlessly and easily to me.**
- **The universal life within me brings me positive results now and in every phase of my life.**
- **My life is unfolding in a perfect and balanced way.**
- **My creator loves me unconditionally.**
- **I surrender my personal will in perfect trust that divine will moves me to my highest good.**
- **I flow effortlessly with the current of life.**

Power-Charging Your Goals

Most people, when asked what they want out of life are quite vague with their answers. You will often hear "I want to be happy", or "I want more money". *Conversations With God, Book I,* suggests that whenever we use the word "want" we are automatically separated from our goal as we are making a statement of lack. By declaring that you want something, you are ultimately stating that you do not have it and this thought form becomes creative by perpetuating the deficiency. When we limit our goal-setting to a statement of need we are not activating the *Law of Concentrated Attention* to our benefit. By defining our goals by what impact the desired outcome would bring upon our senses, we are aiming the laser beam and adding on a powerful charge.

Goals are relative. If you simply state that you want more money, that could be taken to mean having some excess income to spend in your checking account. Being affluent for one person may mean being able to afford to live in a nice apartment, while for another it may mean having his or her own yacht or mansion. Likewise, wanting to be "happy" is a trap; if you can't define what being happy would look, sound and feel like to you, the same behavioral patterns will rule your life. Below is an example of how to power-charge your goals:

GOAL: Getting a better job

I see: People looking at me with respect and admiration
More money in my savings account
Better furnishings in my home
A new car
Myself dressed as a professional

I hear: Positive comments from my loved ones
The praises of my superiors
Congratulations by my fellow workers
The sound of the motor of my new car

I feel: Satisfaction for my progress
The pleasure of being able to give more to my family
The soft leather seat of my new car
The sensation of fine fabrics against my skin

By taking the time to complete the following exercise you will certainly activate the *Law of Concentrated Attention*. The laser beam will hone in on what you desire. You can then build a spiral of belief and activate the *Law of Dominant Effect* by spending a few moments each day seeing, hearing and feeling the attainment of these goals. I suggest that you detach from any expectation of how these goals will actually become reality: they will likely manifest in ways that you could not have planned or imagined!

Power-Charging my Goals
Worksheet

3 month goals: _____
_____
_____
_____
_____

Now break each goal down, according to what you'd like to see, feel, and hear:

I see: _____
_____
_____
_____
_____

I hear: _____
_____
_____
_____

I feel: _____
_____
_____
_____

6-month goals: _____
_____
_____
_____
_____

I see: _____

_____

_____

_____

_____

I hear: _____

_____

_____

_____

_____

I feel: _____

_____

_____

_____

_____

<u>12 month goals:</u> _____

_____

_____

_____

I see: _____

_____

_____

_____

I hear: _____

_____

_____

_____

I feel: _____

_____

_____

_____

_____

5 Year Goals: _____

_____

_____

_____

_____

I see: _____

_____

_____

_____

_____

I hear: _____

_____

_____

_____

_____

I feel: _____

_____

_____

_____

_____

Self-Hypnosis

All hypnosis is self-hypnosis. You go into trance many times a day whether you believe in hypnosis or not. The goal here is to *use* these natural states intentionally rather than be *used* by them. By recognizing and implementing those moments when your subconscious naturally takes the dominant position, you have the power to influence your reactions. For instance, if you find yourself lost in a daydream or extremely agitated, these are crucial moments to be aware of your thoughts. You can cancel out any ideas that are not serving you for your highest good and give yourself an affirmation or positive message. This will neutralize the effect of any negative thought forms or suggestions that are automatically being filed into your subconscious. But it is through your consistent use of the altered state that you can have the most influence over your programming. One of the Rules of Suggestion is *repetition*. Your current habitual patterns were created by redundancy and can only be undone or modified by providing the proper suggestions, given in the appropriate language, in a ritualistic manner. This is the strength of the *21-Day Secret*. Hypnosis is one of the ultimate ways to access the subconscious, as well as, being a totally safe and relaxing experience.

Whether you go to a hypnotherapist, listen to a hypnosis cassette or give yourself the instructions to enter trance, *you* are the director of your experience. No one can make you do something that you are unwilling to do. The state of hypnosis creates a condition in which there is direct access to the subconscious mind, which facilitates the acceptance of suggestion. It is also a very pleasant and natural state when it is produced by intentional methods. When we are hypnotized our minds tend to shift from the logical, critical and analytic mode to one that is holistic, aware, expansive and creative.[33] All of the tools that you will find in your kit are quite potent when used on their own, but the hypnotic state will really amplify the effect.

In order to enter the trance state you need to do some kind of induction. For example, the first technique I offer begins with deep breathing and then you will travel through your body in your mind, turning off a switch in all of the major joints. This is called a *progressive relaxation,* which forms the basis of the majority of hypnotic inductions. There are unlimited ways in which to guide yourself into trance, but you should try to include some kind of focus on each part of your body, instructing it to relax and let go. This will direct your attention inwards and facilitate the passage of suggestion to your subconscious as well as alleviate any build up of stress or tension in your body.

The reason that I am starting you off with the switch technique is that it is so easy to implement. This has made it the most popular technique among my students internationally. I've also included some other ideas that you might find fun and effective. There is no singular way to describe the sensation that one feels in the state of hypnosis as it is such a subjective experience and varies with every individual. As I've pointed out, you have been in and out of unintentional states of hypnosis thousands of times throughout your life and you were not even aware of it. For that reason, you would be hard-pressed to give me a description of what hypnosis feels like. There are certain characteristics and levels of trance that I will describe here, but don't be surprised if you have no discernible symptoms. Intentional hypnosis becomes a collective phenomenon, which means that each time you induce the state, the deeper you go. There are infinite levels to the hypnotic trance. Although you might have experiences that are more superficial during those times that you are preoccupied, the trend will be to spiral into more profound states the more you implement your self-hypnosis.

Some people describe experiencing a generalized relaxation throughout their body, while in others it may be more localized to the head, hands or shoulders. You may find your arms and legs becoming pleasantly heavy, which characterizes the mid-level trance. You could feel as if your body was weightless, or it could be quite lethargic. These sensations are equated more to the deeper states.

My best advice to you is to surrender yourself to the experience. That does not mean that you are giving your power over to any person or thing, but rather, to a natural condition of your mind that can bring forth innumerable benefits. There is no danger of remaining locked in trance or becoming a zombie. If you fall asleep you will just rest for a few moments or throughout the night and wake up feeling very refreshed.

You do not need to *try* to make hypnosis happen. It is an automatic condition that occurs whether you are aware of it or not. The act of trying will only activate the *Law of Reverse Effect*, which will only block you from having an authentic experience.

There are various ways you may use the following self-hypnosis inductions: After choosing the most intriguing one, you may read through it several times and then go through it mentally from memory. However, you will get the most benefit from following it step by step. A very effective solution would be to record the induction on one side of a 60-minute audiocassette, either in your own voice or have someone whose voice you resonate with record it for you. If you are doing the recording for yourself make sure to *speak slowly*. It's probably best that you practice reading through the entire script once or twice. It is also very important that in recording your own tape in your own voice, you convert the suggestions to first person. Every time you see the word *you* replace it with *I*, and when you see the word *your*, replace it with *my*. When having someone else record the meditation it is best that they read it as is, remaining in the second person.

You may listen to your tape either sitting down or lying down in a comfortable position. If you are lying in bed you may very well fall asleep, but you will still receive the benefits of the suggestions. You can even put the tape on at bedtime, however, do try to work with the inductions during the day or when you are most alert for at least five times when you are first starting out. Make sure that you are in a place where you will be uninterrupted for the length of the induction. If you find that you must terminate the meditation before the end, make sure that you give yourself a few moments to process the material before you resume normal activities. Under no circumstances should you listen to your cassette while driving an automobile or while operating any machinery.

Effective self-hypnosis should contain all of the elements of the following formula:

DEEP BREATHING: This should be done without any exaggeration or force, just gentle breaths, in through the nose and out through the mouth. Breathing a few times before you begin will help to oxygenate the brain and stimulate the secretion of endorphins, which are the body's natural tranquilizers. Adding color imagery as you breath intensifies the inward focus. It is best to work with pastels, such as pink, yellow, green and blue. Imagine that you are filling yourself with the positive qualities associated with each color, such as unconditional love for pink, blue for peace, yellow for mental clarity, and green for healing. I also suggest to my clients and students that each intake of breath taps into the infinite source of healing energy in the universe and each release of breath allows any tensions, anxieties or concerns to flow out through the soles of the feet. After about 10 breaths you can go back to regular breathing, just in and out through the nose.

INDUCTION: Either a progressive relaxation of all of the major muscle groups, or some kind of guided imagery that deepens the inward focus. See the following section for some excellent ideas.

POST-HYPNOTIC KEY: Once you have discovered your favorite mode of entering trance you can give yourself a *post-hypnotic key to re-enter trance.* This is simply a phrase or a word which, while hypnotized, you suggest to yourself as meaning rapid trance induction. So, if you use the words "Every time I say or think the phrase *wonderful relaxation* I can deepen my level of hypnosis. Whenever I want to re-hypnotize myself, just by breathing deeply and saying or thinking the phrase *wonderful relaxation* I reenter the hypnotic trance effortlessly and easily", you create a post-hypnotic suggestion to re-hypnotize. This will make it easy for you to enter trance whenever you feel the need to take a mini-vacation or use the *21-Day Secret.* In my tapes and seminars I use the phrase, *"Deep Sleep, deeper sleep, deepest sleep".* You may want to choose a certain word or phrase that has a special meaning to you, such as the name of an archangel, a mantra, your favorite gemstone, or a completely invented word.

DEEPENING TECHNIQUE: If at any time you would like to deepen your level of trance or distance yourself from distractions, use a deepening technique, such as imagining yourself walking down a stairway and going deeper with each step, or going down an escalator or elevator. I have included some deepening techniques later in this section.

IMPLANTING SUGGESTIONS: Here is where you will start implanting the programming that you have created according to the *Rules of Suggestion*. There are two ways to choose from to do this:

1) If you are pre-recording a tape for self-hypnosis, simply read the suggestion onto the tape several times at this point.

2) Remember the *key phrase* that I suggested that you create to identify the tone of your programming? This will work very well as a post-hypnotic. All you have to do is read your script out loud 3 times before you start to use your self-hypnosis. Then say the words, "*All of these ideas and suggestions are symbolized by the phrase...*" At this point you can find a comfortable place and begin your induction process. Once you have implemented a deepening technique and find yourself at a comfortable level of trance, all you have to do is mentally repeat the key phrase about 10-20 times, slowly and with pauses in between. This will automatically feed all of the suggestions that you read out loud into your subconscious mind. Throughout the day you can also use your *key phrase* as a post-hypnotic to gently put you in a relaxed frame of mind and to augment the effect of your programming.

AWAKENING: Within the practice of intentional hypnosis we use the word *"wake up"* just as we use the phrase *"deep sleep"*; even though hypnosis is clearly not a physiological sleep state these words heighten the relaxation aspect of the trance state. When you are ready to come back to full awareness, I suggest that you not do so abruptly, i.e. simply opening your eyes. It is important that you do some kind of ritual to *"put the lid back on your subconscious"*, so to speak. Counting yourself up from one to ten, or imagining that you are climbing up a mini-staircase of five steps are excellent ways to end trance. Make sure to give yourself suggestions that you are completely alert, joyful, and refreshed upon awakening.

In the section on the hypnotic phenomena, you learned that there is an internal time clock in the subconscious mind. You can program yourself to automatically come out of trance after a specified time period, such as 20 or 30 minutes. Or you can use self-hypnosis to take a "cat nap" and suggest that after a 30-60 minute period you awaken as refreshed as if you had slept for a full eight hours.

There are also many good commercial self-hypnosis tapes on the market that will expose you to a variety of different induction techniques. I advise you to avoid the ones that have no words and are called "subliminal" messages, as these have not proven to be valid. However, no pre-packaged suggestions will ever be as effective as those that you create on your own as outlined in the *21-Day Secret.*

Effective Inductions

The Switch Technique

Let's begin by taking a few deep, cleansing breaths. These breaths should be slow and gentle, without any forcing or exaggeration. Inhale gently through the nose, hold for a brief second, then exhale through the mouth. Breathing this way 3-10 times oxygenates the brain and allows for the endorphins, the natural tranquilizers of the endocrine system, to be released throughout your entire body. Continue breathing—in through the nose and out through the mouth. Allow yourself to become more relaxed with each breath. Let yourself go.

Now go back to regular breathing, in and out through the nose, without any paying any particular attention to your breathing pattern. Become aware of your body and find the most comfortable position, either sitting down or lying down, with arms and legs relaxed and uncrossed. Feeling very calm, tranquil, and relaxed.

Focus your attention now on your left foot. On top of the foot is a switch, similar to a light switch on a wall. You may actually see it or just get a sense of it. It is in the "On" position. Now mentally turn that switch to "Off". As you do so, feel any tension, pressure or blockages that you may have been carrying in the foot, toes, toenails, sole and heel just disappear. The skin relaxes, the muscles, tendons, bones and joints relax, as you go deeper and deeper.

Imagine that on your left knee you have a switch. Flip that switch now to the "Off" position and at the same time, feel the relaxation spread from your kneecap to the shin, calf and ankle. Any problem or worries that you may have been carrying in this or any part of your body just evaporates as you let yourself go. You are feeling so calm, tranquil, and relaxed.

Moving up to the left hip, there is another switch, and as you release that switch, feel your entire hip and leg joint relax all the way into the thigh. You are feeling so good as your entire left leg relaxes. Your breathing is calm, steady, and relaxed. There are no problems or worries on your mind.

121

Let's repeat that process on the right side, starting with the right foot—turn that switch from "On" to "Off". Now the right knee. Then the right hip. Both legs are now either very, very heavy—or feeling calm and light—but so, so relaxed.

And now to completely relax the lower part of your body, imagine a switch at the base of your spine. As you release that switch feel a wave of relaxation go down your legs to the back of your heels. There's a switch in the navel center and as you turn that switch off, feel your entire abdominal region soften and relax. That's right, just let yourself go.

On the top of your left hand you have a switch. As you turn that switch off, feel that any tension, pressure, or blockages that you may have been carrying in your hand, palm, fingers and fingernails just disappear. The skin relaxes, the muscles, tendons, bones and joints relax as you go deeper and deeper.

Now on your left elbow, turn that switch off. And at the same time feel the relaxation spread from the elbow to the wrist and any problems or worries that you may have been carrying in that part or any part of the body go out through the hand and evaporate. You are so calm, tranquil and relaxed.

On your left shoulder you have a switch, and as you release it, the upper area of your arm, from the shoulder joint down becomes so loose and limp and relaxed. You are feeling so good as you go deeper and deeper. Repeat this process on the right side starting with the hand...now the elbow...now the shoulder. Both arms are very, very heavy—or feeling calm and light—but so, so relaxed.

There is a switch on the throat and as you turn it off the relaxation spreads throughout your chest and gently relaxes all of your internal organs. There's a very important switch on the back of your neck, as you release it you feel the wave of tranquillity spread out across your shoulders, up into the cranial region, and all the way down your spine, spreading out to the major muscles in the back. Feeling so good now as you let go of any tension, pressure or blockages all along the back.

In between your eyebrows you have a switch and as you turn it off your entire face relaxes. All of the worry lines disappear and your skin rejuvenates as the circulation flows freely into all of your features: your eyelids, your nose, your temples, your mouth, your lips and your jaw—they are so completely relaxed.

The last switch is at the very top of your head, and as you turn that final switch off, you feel your entire head relax. Your mind is clear and free of any distractions. Any thoughts about the past or projects in the next few hours just disappear from your mind. Let yourself go.

The Countdown Method

Start by taking three to ten deep, cleansing breaths—in through the nose and out through the mouth. Return to regular breathing, taking a few moments to concentrate on the process of the air entering and leaving through the nostrils. Then, mentally count down from twenty to one, giving a suggestion for relaxation after each number:

20   *I feel my scalp becoming loose and limp and relaxed.*

19   *The relaxation moves now to my forehead, smoothing away all worry lines or tension, as I go deeper and deeper.*

18   *My eyelids are getting heavier and heavier as all the tiny muscles around my eyes begin to relax.*

17   *The relaxation moves along my entire face, relaxing my temples, cheekbones, mouth and jaw. Each and every muscle gets loose, and limp, and relaxed.*

16   *I feel my throat muscles relax as I go deeper and deeper.*

15   *Going way down as the relaxation moves into my shoulders and my upper back.*

14   *The relaxation moves along my spinal column, spreading out to the major muscles of my back. Feeling so calm, tranquil and relaxed.*

13   *The relaxation moves down along my arms, spreading out to the tips of my fingers as I go deeper and deeper.*

12   *Any noises or movements around me neither bother nor disturb me as I go deeper and deeper.*

11   *My chest muscles relax, all of the spaces between my ribs, my*

heart, my lungs, my stomach are becoming so loose and limp and relaxed.

10　*And feeling that relaxation going into the abdominal cavity, my entire upper body is so relaxed as I go deeper and deeper.*

9　*I let myself go, feeling so calm, tranquil and relaxed.*

8　*The relaxation moves into my hips and moves slowly down my legs.*

7　*I feel so good and totally relaxed; there are no problems or worries on my mind.*

6　*The relaxation moves down my legs, past my thighs, my knees, and into my calves.*

5　*Letting go of any tension. Feeling so calm, tranquil and relaxed.*

4　*Feeling the relaxation spreading out to my feet, along the arches, into my toes.*

3　*Calm, tranquil and relaxed from the top of my head to the tip of my toes.*

2　*Letting go of any tension. Feeling so good.*

1　*Calm, tranquil and relaxed, from the top of my head to the tips of my toes.*

The Magnet Method

Use this method while sitting in a chair or in a recliner. Extend both arms in front of you and then let them rest comfortably on your legs or lap, palms facing up and about six inches apart.

Begin by taking some deep breaths and suggesting to yourself that your eyelids are getting heavier with each breath. Allow them to close and then imagine that there is a magnet in the palm of each hand and that they are pulling together, getting closer with each breath and when your hands meet, a wave of relaxation will begin from the top of your head. Now direct that wave of relaxation from the top of your head to the tips of your toes. Feel that wonderful wave starting at your scalp, deeply relaxing your head, and as that wave moves down over your forehead, feel your facial muscles completely soften and relax as all worry lines disappear. Your features and facial muscles are rejuvenating as this wave of relaxation continues down over your throat, relaxing the muscles of your trachea. This wave continues along the back of your neck and shoulders and goes down along your spine, spreading out to the muscles of your back, your hips and buttocks. Feel this wave of relaxation spread throughout your chest, relaxing all of the internal organs, gently softening the spaces between the ribs as you go deeper and deeper into this wonderful state of hypnotic relaxation, feeling warm, safe and secure. Allow these pleasant feelings to radiate to your abdomen and travel all the way down your legs, relaxing all the muscles, joints and tendons to the very tips of your toes.

Guided Imagery

Take yourself to a place that signifies peace and comfort. This can be indoors or outdoors, but let it be somewhere that inspires you, such as on a beach at sunset, or in a beautiful forest. Make sure that you do not have any fears or apprehensions associated with this scenario. Center yourself within this place by involving your five senses in the experience: What colors or shapes do you see around you? Do you feel the breeze on your face or sand beneath your feet? Do you hear the sounds that surround you in this spot, such as birds chirping, or water rushing over rocks? What are the smells and tastes associated with this locale? The more you integrate your senses, the more you have entered into the subjective realm of your imagination.

One of the guided meditations most enjoyed by clients and students is the following:

Imagine yourself in a canoe, built especially for your body. You are lying down on comfortable cushions, floating downstream on a narrow river, no problems or worries on your mind. You feel the rays of the sun warming your face and body. Your body relaxes more and more with the warmth of the sun as you gently float downstream on this beautiful river, steadily and slowly, extremely safe and secure in your special canoe. You feel the sensation of the water moving under the canoe. This sensation rocks you gently and the sounds of the water lapping against the canoe are like a lullaby, taking you deeper and deeper into a wonderful state of hypnotic relaxation. You see the gorgeous scenery alongside the banks of the rivers – the lush, tropical plants and multi-colored flowers. There is so much greenery and nature around you. The water is a beautiful shade of green and you see the sun rippling on the water. You see the puffy white clouds in the sky, like balls of cotton, contrasting with the intense blue of the sky and golden yellow sun. There is a scent of nature all around you that permeates your senses and you can actually taste the color green. All is peaceful and tranquil as you continue floating downstream in your canoe...

Using these types of scenarios is very enjoyable and useful for developing your imagination. If you are having difficulty bringing up the images, practice with the exercises in the "Guided Imagery" section.

Deepening Techniques

Falling Leaves

Imagine, if you will, that you are in a favorite outdoor place. A spot that represents to you perfect harmony and security; perhaps, by the edge of a brook, in a field of flowers, or on the lawn in front of your house. This can be a real place or one that exists within your imagination. Picture yourself or get a sense that you are lying on grass so soft that it is like green velvet. In this place you are comfortable and safe.

As you relax in this peaceful, outdoor place, visualize or imagine a tree within your range of vision. A leaf is starting to fall to the ground in slow motion and as I count backwards from ten to one, you identify with the leaf as you slowly allow yourself to drift into deeper, hypnotic relaxation. Let yourself go.

10	*Drifting now, deeper and deeper.*
9	*Let yourself go.*
8	*So calm, tranquil and relaxed.*
7	*Each time you go deeper and deeper.*
6	*Like the leaf, softly spiraling down in slow motion.*
5	*Perfectly safe and relaxed.*
4	*Feeling so good.*
3, 2, 1	*Deep sleep, deeper sleep, deepest sleep*

The Cloud Method

Visualize yourself in a favorite outdoor scene: This can be sitting on a beach, floating down a river on a canoe, sailing on a sailboat or standing at the top of a mountain, whatever feels safe and pleasant. Use all of your inner senses to make the scene as real as possible, noticing what you see, hear, taste, smell and feel while involved in your enjoyable surroundings. Then, within the scenery, lie back and look at the sky. Feel yourself becoming very relaxed from head to toe and then feel yourself becoming so free of tension and worries that you become weightless. Soon you float upwards and find yourself floating on the softest, whitest, most luxurious cloud. Allow yourself to relax fully as the cloud gently carries you back down to where you started

Going Down

At any time that you wish to deepen the level of your trance, simply imagine, see or feel yourself going down a flight of stairs or an escalator. Suggest to yourself that each step or movement is taking you one hundred times deeper. There are infinite levels of your personal hypnosis, so you can continue to go down flights until you have achieved a comfortable depth where you are totally focused inward and are not bothered by any distractions.

The Hypno-Thermometer

This will require some visualization capacity. On your mental screen imagine a large thermometer on the wall with the number 100 at the top and 0 at the bottom. The mercury should be a bright color, perhaps blue or red. Each number can be visible, or markings in between increments of ten. Suggest that numbers 100 all the way down to 67 indicate a light, relaxing state of hypnosis; the numbers from 66 all the way down to 34 a gratifying, medium state of hypnosis; and the numbers from 33 all the way down to 0 signify the deepest, most profound state of hypnosis. Notice the number where the mercury has dropped on the thermometer. Now take yourself ten numbers down. And see if you can take yourself even further down. You can even go to sub-zero numerals!

Part IV: Troubleshooting

*Perhaps some of us have to go through dark
and devious ways before we can find the river
of peace or the high road to the soul's destination.*

Joseph Campbell

Advanced Applications

In this section we will target some of the negative attitudes and emotions that are holding you back from realizing your potential and achieving self-esteem. Having explored your tool kit in the previous section, I hope that by now you will have employed some of the valuable tools for learning to relax and modifying behavior. Although it may seem that you should go straight for the deeper issues, I have found from my own experience and years of clinical practice that the first steps should always be "baby" ones. Simply by quieting your mind and relaxing your body, you are doing a tremendous service for yourself! Keep in mind that stress is habitual and can only be counteracted through bypassing the critical factor of the mind.

Another payoff from having started out with altering your behavior before taking on the emotions is an increased sense of personal power. This will fortify you to be able to face some of those deeply ingrained fears and limiting patterns. It takes courage to take on those "head demons" because the critical factor sets us up to always need to be right. Being the creatures of habit that we are, journeying deep into the subconscious and finding out that we have been wrong in our perceptions feels threatening to us. Even if we are ultimately changing those perceptions for more life-affirming ones, all change is scary at first.

In homeopathic medicine there exists what is known as the *healing crisis*. This has also been called the peeling effect: Sometimes we have to get a little worse before we get better, but it doesn't last for long. The toxic material is moving through our bodies and minds and out into the field where it will eventually disperse, but you may experience some increased intensity of emotion for up to a week and maybe even some physical discomfort. Any of these symptoms can be ameliorated through deep breathing, self-hypnosis, and positive messaging.

When painful memories and unhealthy patterns emerge from your subconscious, make sure to give yourself the time and space to assimilate and integrate them. I recommend that you be particularly kind to yourself. This is a good time to pamper yourself, with candles in the bathtub and aromatherapy oils. Give yourself a treat if you feel like it—a margarita, a movie and popcorn, a piece of pecan pie, a massage or maybe that sweater you've been eyeing. And don't hold back if you feel like having a cry-fest. I guarantee that you will feel much better once the toxicity has had a chance to dissipate. You can also expect to feel absolutely wonderful after some of these exercises with no side effects!

If you feel that you are having difficulty processing some particularly traumatic events from the past, don't hesitate to contact a hypnotherapist, counselor, or psychologist to work through them with someone who can give you some unbiased guidance.

As in the *Tool Kit* you can have these exercises read to you or make a personal tape. At the back of the book is a list of the meditations that I have pre-recorded.

Reprogramming the Data Base

We begin the *Troubleshooting* section with the most indispensable technique. In order for your mind to function at its full ability, you need to shut down and delete some of the outdated programs that you have been running. Computers tend to run out of space or operate sluggishly when too many programs are jammed into their memory banks. Once you clear out the negative belief files and non-productive emotional data, you are free to install the most cutting edge programs that can support your mental capacity and spiritual growth.

Your Master Programmer is your Superconscious mind—the aspect of you that holds the vision of your highest potential. This meditation is a collaborative effort between the two of you. Although the Master Programmer sees the big picture and knows what programs no longer serve you, your full agreement is always needed in order to activate the change. This is to honor your free will and free choice. As the biblical saying goes, *"Ask and ye shall receive"*, only when you ask for assistance or give the permission for any deletion or downloading of programs will your Superconscious intervene.

You will be asked to visualize, imagine, or pretend throughout this procedure. If you have difficulty with creating images on your mental screen, I suggest that you work first with the Imagery Exercises in your *Tool Kit* for a few days before doing this meditation. In any event, your capacity to visualize is not the key element in getting significant results from this exercise. What matters most is your *intention*. The intention is the power behind the thought. As you *intend* to release old fears and limiting belief structures you begin to manifest a brand new reality. Some things will change immediately, others may need some more work. Change is a process, not an event.

I had two main sources of inspiration in creating this valuable technique. One was an email that was forwarded to me entitled "Customer Service". Unfortunately, as this was a mass mailing, I cannot properly credit the origin, but it gave me the idea for reprogramming the database. Another source is a wonderful series of books entitled *Life and Teaching of Masters of the Far East* by Baird T. Spalding. These six volumes were written in the early part of this century and contain a vast amount of wisdom.

Begin with several deep breaths, breathing in through the nose, out through the mouth. Let this deep breathing center you and free your mind of any distractions. *Now choose you favorite method of relaxation* (see *Tool Kit* for "Inductions" and "Progressive Relaxation Techniques"), *allowing each and every muscle in your body to become deeply relaxed.* (At this point you can mentally give yourself a post-hypnotic cue to enter easily into the intentional state of hypnosis.)

Now, imagine, visualize or pretend that you are walking in a garden. It is late in the day—an hour or so before sunset. You are alone in this garden, enjoying a very restful stroll and appreciating all of the sights, sounds, and sensations around you. The temperature is very pleasant, neither warm nor cold. Your breathing remains deep, steady and relaxed without you having to pay any particular attention to it. Your blood pressure is completely normal, neither high nor low. You are completely absorbed in the natural beauty that surrounds you. Noises or movements neither bother nor disturb you. Let any random thoughts that come to your mind gently move past you without any attachment. Surrender yourself to the experience of deep, hypnotic relaxation. You are totally safe and protected.

Now, in your garden you will find a gazebo—a kind of open, six-sided structure that is made of latticed wood. Your gazebo might be very simple or rather ornate. Perhaps it's covered with lovely vines and leaves. There are wooden benches built along each of the sides. Take a seat, relax and remain open to all the experiences that await you. You may want to go back to deep breathing if you find that your mind is becoming too busy. Why not breathe in pastel colors—starting with yellow—breathing in through your nose and imagine your entire body becoming infused with beautiful yellow light. Feel yourself filling with the intention to come face to face with your Essence. And now, if you will, just allow the Superconscious aspect of your mind to appear before you. Let it take on any shape, form or figure. Your Master Programmer can manifest as a shape, such as a circle, triangle, or spiral. Or it may be an object of nature, such as a tree or rock.

This Inner Alchemist can appear to you as a wise old teacher, or as an angel. It does not matter what personification your Superconscious takes on as long as you can feel a sense of acceptance and love radiating from the manifestation. If the being or object seems unpleasant to you in any way, reject its presence and ask internally that you be shown a genuine representation of your Higher Self.

As you are now encountering your Master Programmer, I would like you to spend a few moments expressing your goals and aspirations. Let your Superconscious know how you would like to change. Share your visions with the part of you that carries the seed of your particular mission here on earth. Exchange some ideas of what can be done to make your life experience as fruitful and joyful as possible. Let this be a two-way communication, in that your Superconscious is given the opportunity to respond. This is your inner voice, your innate wisdom speaking. (Pause for 1-2 minutes)

Now, thank your Master Programmer. You will re-encounter him or her in a few moments. Exit the gazebo and walk to the very edge of the garden where you will find a bridge. As you cross the bridge you will find yourself in a modern city, filled with many people and modern skyscrapers. Let your intuition guide you to one of the magnificent, tall structures and walk through the glass doors. Immediately across from you is an elevator. Step inside and face toward the front. You are perfectly safe, completely relaxed. The elevator will take you down 20 flights, deep into the foundation of this building. Each time I mention a number, you are going down one level and deepening your level of hypnosis and relaxation. 20-19-18-17 going way, way down 16-15-14-13-12-11 deeper and deeper with every number 10-9-8-7-6-5-4-3-2-1, very deep now, and so relaxed.

The elevator doors open and you enter a large master control room—the kind you see in space centers, with large screens on all the walls and computer consoles throughout. Your Master Programmer is waiting for you. He or she invites you to make yourself comfortable in a very modern recliner in the center of the room. There is a special headrest, which reads all of your brain wave patterns and can reflect your thoughts to you on the screens. There are armrests equipped with buttons at the end, so that you retain total control over the entire procedure. As you rest comfortably in your special recliner, do some deep breathing to center yourself and align with your Master Programmer.

The Master Programmer, your Superconscious mind, takes a seat at the main console. Every step will be explained to you in detail. You will be asked to indicate your acceptance of any phase along the way by pressing one of the buttons at the end of your armrest, or by mentally stating, "I accept."

The procedure is divided into three stages: Processing, Deleting, and Reprogramming. Let's begin stage one by imagining that you are sending a fine mesh net out into your mind field, about 6-12 inches out from your body and encompassing you from head to toe. This net will trap any obsessive thought patterns caught in your field. Allow this net to gather up any distorted images, critical inner dialogue and insecure feelings. Take a few moments to do this. They are now being funneled into the scanner where they must past through the word/ thought processor. As this material is being processed, be aware of how many judgements you have been carrying around within your field. You might even see them flashing on the screen in front of you. Judgments about your self-worth. Judgments about other people. Judgments about the world. All of these negative ideas tend to reach out and manifest difficult and limiting experiences. Make a decision now. Are you ready to have all of those judgments processed out of your field? Push that button on your armrest, or say, "I accept." Breathe deeply for a few moments now. Notice any changes or alterations in your energy field. Perhaps you feel lighter now, or you may be aware of certain colors pulsating around you. You may even experience a pleasant vibrating sensation.

Send that net out once again, but this time extend it beyond the boundaries of the control room and even beyond the building, out into the city. This time the net is gathering in all of the collective thoughts that have influenced your opinion of yourself and sense of belonging or isolation in the world. Thought forms of the consensus reality are being trapped in the net and they are mainly fears. Fear of not being

135

good enough. Fear of not fitting in. Fear of not living up to society's expectations. Fear of not being considered a worthwhile citizen of the planet. Fear of your fellow human beings.

Are you ready to have all of those collective fears processed out of your field? Push that button on your armrest, or say, "I accept." Breathe deeply for a few moments now. Notice any changes or alterations in your energy field.

Very good. Now we move on to stage two. Your Master Programmer is running a ScanDisk on all of the current programs operating on your mind's hard drive. Many of the programs are obsolete or are incapacitating the overall performance of your hard drive. They are coming up one by one on the screen and you will be asked to make a decision on each one. Guilt: notice any images, feelings, internal dialogues or sensations around the Guilt program. Guilt is an invalid emotion. There is nothing that you have done that you cannot make right in a reasonable period of time. So much of what you feel guilty about has nothing to do with you—it's just the program you came with. Do you want to delete it? Press that button. A prompt is coming up on the screen. It says: "Are you ready to delete it?" Pressing that button alerts the Master Programmer that you have agreed to the deletion of the Guilt program.

The next program is Hate. Notice any images, feelings, internal dialogues or sensations around the Hate program. Hate is a fear-based emotion. It is a reaction that you have to feeling that you are not good enough. It is your way of defending yourself from the many real and imagined injustices of life. But as you realize and accept that everything that you have ever gone through has served to teach you and to prepare you for life's challenges, you have the option of letting go of hate. You were not born with hate, it's just something that got programmed into you. Do you want to delete it? Press that button. A prompt is coming up on the screen. It says: "Are you ready to delete it?" Pressing that button alerts the Master Programmer that you have agreed to the deletion of the Hate program.

Several sub-files to Hate and Guilt are coming up on the screen now. They are Resentment, Envy, Bitterness, Low Self-Esteem, and

Selfishness. They have been operating in the background and infusing your Mind Field with a very low energy vibration. All of these programs have self-perpetuated as they continue to bring in the very experiences that they represent. Take a few moments to consider how those programs may have been restraining your growth. If you are ready to delete all of these invalid files, press that button. Verify your choice by pressing it once again. Take a few moments to rest and breathe deeply as the toxicity is released from your mind and from your energy field. Be aware of any sensations, emotions, or feelings. If anything uncomfortable comes up, just breathe through it.

You have completed the first two stages of the procedure. We are now in the re-programming phase. You are doing quite well. Your Master Programmer is now ready to install the first of two major programs. The first is Forgiveness.exe. By agreeing to install Forgiveness.exe you are allowing the principle of love to send out divine vibrations. You are releasing the storehouse of all the hidden treasures, potential, and gifts of your mind. The Forgiveness program will help all of the other files to run smoothly. Breathe some pink light all way down to your heart and allow it to open. As you breathe out, make your decision. Are you ready for the installation of Forgiveness.exe to take place? Are you truly willing to forgive yourself and others and release a tremendous burden from you mind, heart, body, and energy field? Good. More deep breathing now. As Forgiveness fully downloads throughout your system, notice the effect on any other programs you have running currently.

Finally, you are ready for the Meta Program. This contains directories of all of the highest and most noble attitudes, virtues and habits to support you on your Life Path, such as Self-Esteem, Peace, Wisdom, Love, Truth, Compassion, Trust, and Purpose. All of these traits and behaviors will be stored in your brain cells so that you may access them at any time. You were born with this program, but you are now receiving the most cutting-edge, upgraded edition. The path has been cleared so that your Meta Program can operate effortlessly and effectively. Do you accept installation of the Meta Program now? Are you open and willing to have all the files downloaded onto your hard drive? Just rest now for a few moments as this comprehensive pro-

gram is being downloaded into your mind by your Superconscious. (Pause for 60 seconds). *Congratulations. Installation has been successful. You can now expect your programs to run more smoothly and to generate greater capacity from your hard drive.*

Now that your mind and field have been cleared of distorted images, faulty perceptions, negative beliefs, and self-criticism you may open the channels to a clearer communication with your Master Programmer. Feel free to access his or her wisdom to guide and assist you through the many crossroads and decisions of life. So many doors are opening to you from this day forward. You are living your life joyously and beautifully free. Just as the seed knows that within itself it has the power to express its maximum possibility, your Superconscious holds the vision of your highest potential. You are never alone with this guidance and unconditional support. Notice any images, thoughts or feelings coming up or flashing on your mental screen. These are visions of your highest potential—where you can take your life by working hand in hand with your Superconscious.

At any time you feel that you may be inadvertently being programmed with negative or counter-productive files, make sure to re-visit the control room. Sometimes just by being around pessimistic people your mind field can take on some of their thought forms. By returning to the control center from time to time you are performing a kind of mental and spiritual hygiene. For now, at the count of ten you will come back to full awareness, feeling gloriously alive, alert and well-balanced.

1-2-3-4-5-6-7-8-9-10.

Raising Permission Levels

Consider the various aspects of your life. Do you feel fulfilled in the area of career? Have you achieved a level of satisfaction in your relationships, romantic and otherwise, in that you feel loved and appreciated? How is your health, or your levels of energy and well-being? Have you been able to provide yourself with certain luxuries of life that you long for, such as travel or free time?

Permission levels can be likened to an internal barometer, or unconscious control mechanisms that modulate the amount of bliss, well-being, success, and love we permit ourselves. They are ultimately the results of the programming that we have received in our childhood, but they operate below our conscious awareness.

From my observations, how we experience life is directly related to our permission levels. Here are some examples:

High Bliss PL's: can go through several days or weeks on an even keel and generally enjoys life.
Low Bliss PL's: daily or weekly mood swings and feelings of victimization.

High Well-Being PL's: rarely gets sick, good overall vital energy and knows how to take some "down-time" to relax.
Low Well-Being PL's: feels guilty about relaxing or doing something for self. Usually has to get sick in order to "allow" time off.

High Success PL's: Works at something they love, on a schedule that best suits them.
Low Success PL's: Hates their job, feels imprisoned by the schedule, fear of taking risks.

Dissatisfaction with your present circumstances and a sense of frustration at not being able to achieve your desires are immediate red flags that your low permission levels have been obstacles to achieving your desires. Your permission levels can be high in some areas and lower in others. The good news is that they can all be raised by conscious intention!

While it is certainly possible to raise your permission levels (see the exercise below) I feel that it's important to caution you that higher permission levels require greater levels of responsibility. For instance, raising your permission levels for health and well-being means that you have to come to terms with what is non-negotiable for maintaining a vigorous body. Allowing for more satisfactory relationships (love) means that you have to acknowledge that it is your responsibility to commit to better communication skills.

First, we'll start with a technique for measuring the degree of your overall permission levels. Then, I'll share a simple exercise for raising them through intention; however, I recommend that you start with an increase of 5-20 degrees. Naturally it would be ideal to have your permission levels at 100%, but that doesn't mean that you are ready for that dramatic of a change in your life, or that you are currently equipped to handle the heightened responsibility.

Important note: Allow the number that appears in this exercise to come from your subconscious. In other words, don't project the number that you *want* to see. From earlier chapters you should have learned that the gap between what you consciously *desire* and what your subconscious mind *believes* is as wide as the Grand Canyon!

Close your eyes and take a few deep breaths, allowing any distractions, preoccupations, discomfort or worries to disappear. Feel your mind and body relax more with every breath.

Imagine that on the wall in front of you is a gigantic thermometer with the number 100 at the top and going down in increments of 10 all the way to 0. Make this image very real to you.

Now, in your imagination, look away from the thermometer. Ask internally "What is my current overall permission level?" Remember, this is not what you would like it to be or hope to achieve, but honoring where you actually are at this moment. Now count mentally to three and look back at the thermometer.

A pink mercury line will have risen to a certain number. Look closely and identify that number. How do you feel about it?

Would you like to raise that number? If so, take a deep breath and as you exhale allow the pink mercury to rise 5 degrees. Do you feel good about this level? Are you open to all of the gifts and blessings of this level? Are you willing to accept the responsibility that accompanies this raise? Allow this increase to imprint on a cellular level, throughout all the aspects of your being (You may repeat this until you have achieved the level in which you would like to remain for the time being).

Now repeat the above steps for each of the following areas:

Bliss.   Well-being.   Success.   Love.

We will continue to work with raising your permission levels in my new workbook, *A Year of Positive Habits.*

The Wheel of Life

Finding Balance in Your Life

Life is a circle. A circle represents 360 degrees. There are six basic components to our lives, which are outlined in the following chart: Mental, Physical, Spiritual, Career, Family, and Culture. In order to maintain an equal flow of energy (thus, a feeling of balance) we need to divide our time equally between each area.

Most of us concentrate the majority of our attention on two or three areas, creating a lopsided effect. Have you ever wondered why you felt so off-center? As you can see from the example below, this person is leading a rather unbalanced life, leaning more towards career and advancement, while virtually ignoring family, social and spiritual needs. This will have major consequences down the road even though he now seems to be operating on automatic pilot. Even the emphasis on his physical body is weak. This could be remedied by being more active, perhaps by joining a gym or participating on a sports team on the weekends. That could even satisfy some of his social needs. He might want to take his family to an art museum or exhibit. Spending some time in nature could get him into a more contemplative and spiritual place.

Take a few moments to map out your own wheel by jotting down all of the activities that you regularly do in a four-week period under the appropriate division: Sunday dinner at my mother's under "Home and Family", or spend 15 minutes twice a week on the treadmill under "Physical".

After you get a visual image of where your own wheel of life is lacking balance, see my suggestions on how to establish more equilibrium in the underdeveloped segments of the pie chart. You might find many surprises as you work on this exercise. The more you view yourself from a holistic perspective, the more you will recognize that all your parts need to be integrated in order to feel and function as a conscious and whole being.

These are examples of activities that you can weave into your schedules, in order to balance out your wheel of life. Feel free to come up with your own ideas!

Physical

Take up a sport
Go for a walk
Go swimming
Watch fat intake
Dance on the weekends
Rest more

_____
_____
_____
_____

Mental

Read books
Study a language
Take a college course
Learn a new skill
Increase your vocabulary
Do puzzles

_____
_____
_____
_____

Spiritual

Read poetry
Learn to meditate
Visit a new church or temple
Read a new age book
Donate/volunteer your time
Be in nature

_____
_____
_____
_____

Home/Family

Spend quality time
Play more with kids
Help kids with homework
Travel on weekends
Study something together
Practice communicating

_____
_____
_____
_____

Culture

Go to museums
Learn a "hobby"
Do volunteer work
Go to the library
Visit more with friends
Try ethnic foods

_____
_____
_____
_____

Career/Money

Take courses
Make a budget
Update your resume
Investigate new opportunities
Learn how to invest
Get specific training

_____
_____
_____
_____

Here's an extra chart. Why not try this again in about 3 months. Has the overall composition changed much? Be sure to make copies and have your family members and friends try this exercise.

The Garden of Beliefs

Guided Meditation

The purpose of this guided exercise is to return you to the pre-existence state when you planned what you would do with the gifts of this lifetime. Let's suppose that before coming into life you had the opportunity to chart out your biography: your life purpose, your mission, your accomplishments, your talents and your contributions to the world.

We will use the metaphor of a garden in which you used careful thought and planning to make the most of the space and conditions available to you. Let's return now to that garden and remind you of your original blueprint and noble intentions.

You may record this meditation for yourself or have someone read it to you slowly. This is also available as a professionally recorded tape.

Find a comfortable place, lying down or sitting down. Make sure that you have nothing crossed so that you do not block the energy flow. Begin by taking several deep breaths, gently breathing in through the nose—a slight pause—and then out through the mouth. As you breathe in, fill yourself from the infinite source of divine wisdom and healing. As you breathe out, let go of any tensions, resistance or anxiety. Allow your body to relax more with every gentle breath.

(Use your post-hypnotic cue here to enter trance)

Imagine now a stairway with ten wide, marble steps. The banisters are made of wrought iron in a beautiful floral pattern. As you walk down each step, feel yourself becoming more deeply relaxed. In fact, each stair will take you 100 times deeper into your hypnotic relaxation. When you reach the last step you are 1,000 times deeper— the deepest, most delicious trance that you have ever experienced.

10 *Take that first step down. 100 times more deeply relaxed.*

9 *Feeling so calm, tranquil and relaxed, from the top of your head to the tips of your toes.*

8 *Let yourself go. No problems or worries on your mind.*

7 *Going deeper now.*

6 *Deep sleep is moving deep inside your body. Your mind drifts into a peaceful state of tranquility.*

5 *Halfway there now. So calm, tranquil and relaxed.*

4 *Peaceful, deep, relaxing sleep.*

3 *Resting now from the top of your head to the tip of your toes.*

2 *Feeling so good, so calm and relaxed.*

1 *1,000 times deeper. Deep sleep, deeper sleep, deepest sleep.*

Imagine yourself now entering a beautiful garden. This place is so unique and tranquil that if feels like a sanctuary to you—a place that is free of any worries or problems. There is a familiar feeling to this place. As you take a few moments to become aware of your surroundings you feel layers of fears, limitations, negative feelings just evaporating, being lifted by the gentle breezes and carried away to a place of renewal and transformation. You begin to feel lighter, more authentic, as if you were tuning into your true essence.

As you walk deeper into this garden, you become more deeply relaxed. It seems increasingly more familiar to you. You are becoming more convinced that you have been to this place before—long ago— perhaps before you began to experience the physical world. A time when you were a spirit—pure and innocent—preparing for your arrival to the physical world. You now let your intuition be your guide as you enter more deeply into the garden, to a special corner. This place is very private and seems to belong to you. You feel as if you were coming home, to a much-loved and comfortable place.

In this particular area of the garden there is a plot of earth planted with flowers and greenery. Now you recognize this place. The greenery and vegetation represent all of your wishes, longings, ambitions and intentions that you prepared to take with you into the physical world. Every flower and plant is unique. Each flower and plant represents something very dear and private to you – something that you fervently desire in the deepest recesses of your heart and in the very fibers of your being.

However, weeds have overgrown this small plot of land, tangling all of the stems and suffocating the roots, causing the plants and flowers to wither away. No longer does this greenery blossom or flourish. How sad to see all of your dreams wilting and drying up, abandoned and forgotten.

I invite you now to restore your garden. The weeds represent all of the negative and erroneous beliefs that were sown within your early years of development. It's time to get rid of those weeds that no longer serve you for your Highest Good. Your herbicide is your dynamic willpower and your sincere desire to excel.

147

You get on your knees now and begin to work in your garden with all of your tools. These are the resources that you have gathered in your lifetime. Your weeding hoe represents your ability to distinguish between the beneficial herbs and the useless weeds: The belief systems that serve you well and those that stifle your growth and potential. Your watering can represents your faith and inspiration, which help your garden flourish.

You notice that you are carrying seeds with you and you place them deep into the earth. These new seeds are the positive belief systems that you are claiming as a mature and self-actualized adult; beliefs that support your realizing all of your dreams; belief systems that generate attitudes, feelings, thoughts and action congruent with all of your finest aspirations and intentions.

Here in your garden you are in touch with Nature. Let your goals and dreams blossom and flourish. Take your time in the garden. Enjoy these special moments in silence.

(Pause for several minutes)

Your internal representations are being altered in these moments. The circumstances of your life are changing from this moment forward. You have implanted your subconscious with life-affirming belief systems that are the new commanders of your destiny. From this moment forward you are creating a new life history. These positive beliefs are activating your nervous system. These positive beliefs are manifesting your goals every moment of your life. You walk, talk, think and act out in accordance with these new and positive belief systems. You release the past and embrace the present and the future. Your garden has been replanted and you are experiencing a rebirth. You are firmly on the path to achieving your goals.

It is time now to leave this garden, but feel free to come back to this place anytime you desire, whether it is to tend your plants, walk in nature, or to be in silence and tranquility.

As I count now from one to ten, you walk back up the stairs and feel yourself coming back to full awareness, feeling wonderfully good from head to toe, refreshed and alert.

1-2-3-4-5-6-7-8-9-10

Discovering the First Thought

Don't be discouraged if you haven't been able to change a behavior in a 21-day cycle. It's possible that you have a certain perception at the core of a belief system that is contradictory to your goal. This exercise can take you to the root of what may be blocking you from unveiling your true potential.

Remember that the majority of your programming occurred in the first dozen or so years of your life. This is when you established your basic attitudes about your self-image, personal security, money, success, morals, and values. As an adult you have learned many new things about life and the world, yet those early belief systems still dominate the dynamics of your subconscious mind. A desire to change rarely carries sufficient strength to combat the prevailing belief system. Therefore, the first thought will reign supreme unless it is uncovered and challenged. This guided meditation is designed to uncover the origin of your blocked desires and give you the opportunity to modify or change the first thought so that it supports your present goals.

I recommend that you have a specific intention in mind while practicing this exercise rather than looking for generalities. In other words, don't just go in with the intention of finding out what is wrong with your life. Search for a particular situation in your life that you have felt powerless to change. For instance, if you find it difficult to leave an abusive relationship, focus on what thought or attitude may have contributed to this behavior. Maybe you were told that you must martyr yourself to the relationship at all costs, or perhaps that leaving a marriage could threaten your immortal soul. I am not suggesting that these original programs are false, only that *you* have the option to make an informed choice as to whether they are serving you at present for your highest good. I feel that it's important to advise you that not all issues can be resolved or discovered through this method. There may be some areas that your subconscious is intentionally blocking if you haven't yet reached a place in your development where you are ready to face them head on. You also may need to have an impartial witness or "tour guide" to take you back to these events through hypnotic age regression in order to truly unearth the causes of your stumbling blocks.

Just approach this technique in a very open and surrendered way, trusting that whatever is revealed is what is meant to be.

Begin by taking a few, deep, cleansing breaths. As you breathe in feel yourself absorbing support from the universe for the realization of your desires. As you breathe out, release any attachments that you have to any old thought forms or behavioral patterns. Imagine yourself surrounded by a clear, white light with golden sparkles. This light supports and protects you throughout this experience. (Enter trance now by giving yourself a pre-programmed suggestion or a post-hypnotic key at this point. In order to deepen your relaxation and heighten your capacity for recall, use the progressive relaxation technique or induction of your choice)

Your mind is clear and free of any distractions. Any thoughts about the past or projects in the next few hours just disappear from your mind. Let yourself go. I would like you now to get a sense of yourself, your entire body, as being very small, no bigger than 4 inches tall. You are standing beneath a dome, surrounded by windows on all sides. You may see these windows perhaps decorated with exquisite stained glass, like the ones in the ancient European cathedrals, or you may experience the windows as ultra-modern and clear. Take a few moments to create this special space. (Pause) This dome represents your head, the entranceway to the discovery of your first thoughts. Welcome. You are now on the inside looking out. If this is all new for you, just allow yourself the experience of accessing your inner self. At any time that you wish to end this session, you may simply take a deep breath and open your eyes. You are safe, calm, tranquil and relaxed from the top of your head to the tip of your toes.

This is the control center. Any movement that you make, any intention to make that movement, any impulses you may feel, and any information that filters through your five senses will originate from this center. You have a mind, both conscious and unconscious. You have a brain, divided into two hemispheres. You have a cerebral cortex, which stores all of the programming that you have ever received. And you have a nervous system, which is the message center to your entire body. The lines of communication are the neurotransmitters that send bil-

151

lions of messages to every cell in your body. What you think, what you say, what you feel, and what you desire will all be communicated by these neurotransmitters to your cells; they are the genies that carry out all of your commands.

Now imagine, if you will, an elevator at the center of the dome. It can have glass doors like the one in luxury hotels, or metal doors like a generic building elevator. There is a door in front and in back. I invite you now to enter the elevator, facing front. The elevator is moving straight down, very slowly and taking you deeper as you feel yourself being pulled into this profound state of hypnotic relaxation. So calm, so tranquil and relaxed, moving down, going deeper, no problems or worries on your mind. Let yourself go. The elevator is coming to a stop. The front door opens and you are inside of your physical body at the level of your heart. As you step out, get a feeling for your surroundings. Be aware, if you will, of what sights, sounds, and textures encircle you.

This is your heart center—representing your potential to feel bliss, joy and ecstasy. The area that generates your capacity to love and to feel compassion. The center that lifts you above your survival instincts into the realm of deep feeling and humanitarian deeds. It is here that your heart's desires begin their ascent into manifestation.

The color green is associated with the heart center. Make yourself comfortable here by imagining yourself sinking into a cushy, green couch. Or wandering through a lush, verdant rain forest. Or lying down on a soft, velvety lawn. Go deeper now, much deeper.

Think about a desire that feels unfulfilled—something that you have wanted for a long time but seems to elude you. Say to yourself, silently, "I have the desire to..." Let that statement resonate for a few moments in the space of your heart center. Notice any emotions, feelings, physical sensations or sounds that may come up. You may want to repeat the statement a few times. "I have the desire to..." Answer the following questions to yourself:

When you state your desire, are you aware of any constrictions in that center?

Do you feel peaceful and/or hopeful, or are you experiencing

152

any fear or anxiety?

Do you perceive any darkening of the colors around you?

Does your desire feel unattainable or beyond your grasp at this time?

If the answer to all of the above questions was "No", then you are ready to move on to the next step. Just rest a few moments and relax as your desire is transmitted and recorded in every cell and fiber of your heart center.

If you answered "Yes" to any of the above, understand that your desire possibly does not resonate with this vital area of your being. Perhaps you have desired something that is not in alignment with your true nature, or maybe it was something that you were taught that you should want. This desire might seem very important to your mind, but trust that your heart center knows what serves you for your highest good. Perhaps this is not the optimal timing for the realization of your desire or for you to explore this issue at a deeper level. However, the choice is yours. You may come back to full awareness at this point, or continue on the journey.

Once again you enter the elevator. The doors close and you continue going deeper as the elevator moves down. At the count of six you will find yourself at the next destination. Feel yourself become more deeply relaxed with every number. 1-2-3-4-5-6

The elevator is coming to a stop. The front door opens and you are inside of your physical body at the level of your diaphragm, slightly above the navel. As you step out, get a feeling for your surroundings. Be aware, if you will, of what sights, sounds, and textures encircle you.

This is your solar plexus—the muscles associated with your breathing. This center is the focal point of your will power, where you carry the energy necessary to accomplish your goals. The seat of your self-esteem and strength of character. It is here that you generate the vitality to bring your desires into manifestation.

Imagine, if you will, a bright disc of golden light, like a miniature sun. Get a sense that this brilliant yellow sphere is filling the entire area between your breastbone and navel. Expand the sensation into every cell and fiber of your being as you once again focus on your desire. Now, state your intention, either verbally or mentally, that you seek to find what is blocking you from your desire. You are completely willing to know the truth.

Now I would like you to create an image of an energetic replica of yourself. This would simply be your magnetic field, so it requires no features or detail – just an outline of your body. This is the part of you that carries your thoughts, your impressions, your memories—it is the liaison between you and the external world. It remembers all that you have experienced and learned. All that you have been told.

Imagine your energy body wrapped loosely in layers of gauze. In your mind grab the end piece, which is hanging loosely from one shoulder and unwrap one full layer. Take a deep breath now and notice what feelings, memories or impressions come up. (Pause) Keep unwrapping layers until you encounter the first thought—the experience or statement that formed the basis of your erroneous belief system. When you have a clear sense or image, ask yourself the following question:

Am I willing to let this belief go?

If the answer is "Yes", imagine that you are sending the thoughts, feelings, attitudes and perceptions associated with this belief system down a drain, seeing the energy swirling in a spiral and disappearing. Take a deep breath and let go through the soles of your feet. Now, make a statement in the affirmative that replaces the first thought. Tell your subconscious mind what you now hold as the new belief system. Relax deeply for a few moments as this new conviction takes root in your subconscious mind.

If you answered "No", ask your subconscious to give you an idea of what you still need to do or learn in order to be free of this limiting belief system. Ask when you might be more prepared to move through your blockages. Relax deeply as you surrender to this higher knowledge.

Preparing now to come back to full awareness at the count of five, feeling so refreshed, alert and positive about your existence. 1-2-3-4-5. Coming up with a beautiful sense of well-being. Wide awake.

154

Post-Hypnotics

Post-hypnotics are suggestions given in the (hypnotic) trance state, intended for the subconscious to act upon and carry out in the waking state. They are commands to be put into action in our conscious, normal state. Another word for post-hypnotic is "cue".

For instance, if you are using self-hypnosis to eat more slowly, you would implant a command into your suggestion, such as *"Every time I place food into my mouth, my normal chewing reaction slows down 50%. I automatically chew my food more slowly and completely before I swallow. Food placed in my mouth immediately sends the signal to my chewing reflex to SLOW DOWN."* Thus, the subconscious—ruler of most of the body's functions—has been directed to respond automatically when you start eating.

Here are some examples of how you can maximize your hypnotic suggestions by post-hypnotic cues, but feel free to experiment with some of your own innovations. You will find more in the "Glove Anesthesia" and "Healing and Pain Control" chapters.

Breathing for Fear, Stress, Anxiety and Overcoming Cravings

Dr. Andrew Weil, a very respected physician in the field of alternative medicine, has stressed that if he were to recommend one thing that could maintain good health and give greater access to spontaneous healing, it would be to work with our breath: "...breath is the link between body and mind, between the conscious and subconscious minds. It is the master key to the control of emotions and to the operations of the involuntary nervous system...Turning your attention to your breath...puts you in conscious touch with your vital, nonphysical essence."[34] One of the most powerful cues you can give to your subconscious is to signal an increased awareness of your breathing.

"Any time that I feel anxiety (or fear, stress, panic, or cravings), I automatically take three deep breaths of air and I feel completely at ease and relaxed. My brain is supplied with sufficient oxygen for me

155

to find the solution to any problem, large or small. Three deep breaths of air make me feel as if I am standing under a waterfall of healing energy and light."

The Control Key for Fear, Panic Attacks, Stress and Anxiety

This involves creating a stimulus-response pattern. By giving this post-hypnotic suggestion you will be programmed to automatically squeeze the dominant hand, and then open and close it several times whenever you are faced with a stressful situation or the object of your fear. In *Operation and Structure* you learned that once a stimulus is programmed to activate the flight or fight syndrome in your primitive mind it will always invoke the same reaction. By transferring the reaction to your hand you could eventually break the circuit and liberate yourself of the repetitive and ultimately debilitating flight or fight response. This is a great one to do if you stress out while driving in heavy traffic or on the freeway.

"Any time I feel any tension (or fear, etc.) I automatically begin to squeeze my right (or left) hand. I then slowly open and close my hand several times, thinking or saying the word, "Control". Any tensions (or fears, etc.) instantly disappear. I am completely safe. My body relaxes from the top of my head down to my toes."

The Comfort Zone for Depression, Fear, Grief and Anxiety

This is a technique in which you combine a comfortable object or essence with suggestion so that by touch or smell you will feel an instant relief. You may want to twirl your favorite ring around your finger or grasp a necklace, charm, or key chain that you can easily access. The sensation of the object can have a very calming effect.

The fastest route to the subconscious mind is through the sense of smell. Aromatherapy oils, which are derived from flowers, plants, spices, fruits, and trees, are exceptional mood enhancers. Find a natural food store or supplier of organic essences in your neighborhood and sniff a variety of the essential oils to find one that is particularly pleasing to you. (Or see the appendix in the back) You may also find a blend of oils that especially appeals to you. Valerie Worwood, considered to be one of the definitive experts in the field of aromatherapy describes different personality types according to resonance with certain groups of oils in *The Fragrant Mind*.[35]   In this book she also prescribes combinations of oils that can help relieve various emotional states, such as resentment, loneliness, and guilt. You can also program any essential oil to give you the effect as directed by your suggestion.

"At the onset of any tension (fear, anxiety, panic, etc) I reach for my (object) or (essential oil). By holding this item (or smelling this essence) I am instantly transported to a place of security and comfort. Feeling (or smelling) this object relaxes my body and mind and gives me the peace and tranquility to deal with any situation."

Inner Guidance for Intuition and Decision-Making

Remember, intuition means being tutored from within. There is always information available to help you make decisions or choose a more suitable path. It's just a matter of trusting that you are not alone and that you live in a benevolent universe. By establishing a code of communication with your Superconscious mind you can learn to interpret the signals and take a course of action. Although your Superconscious and subconscious minds conspire to help you in the greatest possible way to achieve your mission and bring forth all of your potential, you are ultimately the one who has free will. Guidance from within is just a way of giving you compassionate options, but the choice is always yours.   In this technique you can program a certain internal signal to let you know when a situation is favorable, such as a warm sensation around your heart. When a situation is not as it seems or presents a potential danger, you can ask for a different signal, such as feeling a cold sensation in the solar plexus (diaphragm) area. Make sure to express your gratitude for this open channel of communication.

"I am now openly accepting the collaboration of my Superconscious (or Inner Guide). I welcome your assistance in my life. In order to establish a direct route of communication between us, I ask that you give me the following cues or signals. When something or someone is trustworthy or favorable, or if this situation is one that serves me for my higher purpose, please send me this signal _____.
When I am in danger, or if someone can't be trusted, or a situation arises that would not be productive for my growth, please let me know by _____. Thank you in advance for alerting me in these ways. I am so grateful to have this bond of trust and communication between us.

Learning to Forgive

We've all been hurt by somebody in our lives. Often the person who hurt us did it without any bad intentions, but rather from a state of ignorance. Or maybe their own faulty programming, passed on generation by generation like a chain, compelled their unjust behavior. As Louise Hay puts it "we are all victims of victims".[36] By learning to forgive, you are not resigning yourself to mistreatment or allowing the person(s) that wounded you to have unlimited access to your emotions. You are severing an energetic bond and freeing yourself of a two-way channel of damaging forces. By releasing the other party, you allow more light into your mind, illuminating your path. You will feel lighter and freer.

What was done to you was probably terribly unfair and extremely traumatic, but by holding onto resentments you are only prolonging the agony. Remember the "what if" game I told you about in *Power Supply*? Why not practice a few "what if's" as you reflect on your perception of what has happened. Here are some possible questions you may want to consider:

What if the person who hurt me was someone who had also been deeply hurt and acted out of ignorance or unconsciousness?

What if my being hurt that way served some Master Plan designed to help me discover more of my true nature?

What if by forgiving this person or situation I would be free to move forward in my life? Where would I like to see myself once I am lighter and freer?

What if, by forgiving, I would feel a closer relationship to the Divine? What gifts, blessings, and benefits might I receive as a result of taking this higher road?

What I have found after years of clinical practice is that the one who is the most difficult to forgive is ourselves. Without forgiveness, there is a serious deficiency of self-love and your life will feel out of balance. Even if you achieve some success or happiness in one area of your life, another one will suffer as a result of the punishment that you will be unconsciously inflicting upon yourself. You can practice this exercise on yourself.

Don't be discouraged if at first you find it very hard to mentally communicate to the "perpetrator of the crime". Anger is a natural protective instinct and must be processed before we can truly forgive. It took Karen three weeks to be able to "face" her enemy in a rational way. If you are still carrying anger towards this person, there is no bypassing that stage to go on to boundless forgiveness. Spend some time venting—you are only doing this in your imagination, however, you will be releasing the stored up energy. Only then will you open up to a more productive way of perceiving the situation.

Make sure to do this exercise with each person in your past that you are carrying unresolved issues with. You may want to start with someone that provokes the least rage, or you may decide to go after the major culprit right from the start.

In some of these relationships, you may never have to physically face or encounter the individuals again, but you will be free of their tyranny over your life as well as the destructive emotions that are dissipating your energies. In other cases, you may find that these techniques have magically opened the door to a conversation that can be carried out in a mature way, without accusations and intense emotional charge.

Forgiveness Exercise

Visualize or imagine the person(s) whom you resent or hate surrounded by a white/gold-colored light. Allow any feelings or emotions to come up without attempting to change or suppress them by willpower. Now imagine that a rose-colored thread or tube connects your heart to theirs. Begin to communicate with this person through the heart thread, letting them know exactly why you are upset with them. From time to time you may want to sit in silence and be aware of any "explanations" or "responses" that may be coming from them. Continue the dialogue until you feel that the intensity of your emotions begin to dissipate.

Once you feel a sense of release, imagine that there is a current of peace, harmony, love and forgiveness flowing between the two of you. Then either mentally or verbally express to this person that you forgive him/her and that you are releasing them to their higher good. When you feel complete you may gently withdraw the rose-colored thread. Let them drift away, still surrounded by the white/gold light of divine protection.

Continue practicing this exercise with each person that you resent, until you are easily able to let them drift away, without any residual anger. Should you find the act of forgiveness to be particularly difficult, ask for the guidance and intervention of the Supreme Being with whom you most resonate.

e Anesthesia

Pain Control through the Power of Your Mind

One of the greatest treasures of our subconscious components is the capacity to alter our perception of pain. Prescription painkillers and over-the counter analgesics certainly come in handy, but on the downside are the issues of dependency and side effects. Not only will your body benefit from this skill; you will also acquire a sense of self-sufficiency and power over your life as well. The phenomena of glove anesthesia or analgesia is one of the simplest to execute, requiring only a medium trance. The following induction is designed to take you effortlessly into this mid-level state, called *catalepsy*, which is characterized by a generalized feeling of relaxation with localized heaviness in the extremities, head, neck or shoulders.

You may want to practice some of the basic inductions in the *Tool Kit* section until you feel proficient in entering a comfortable state of self-hypnosis before attempting to produce this phenomenon. Nevertheless, this is easier than you can imagine, so don't feel that you have to be an expert first. If you feel intimidated by creating this technique on your own, contact a local certified hypnotherapist, as this is something that they would have learned in their basic training.

Once you have relaxed into catalepsy you will give suggestions that one of your hands (I recommend that you choose either the dominant hand, or the one that is most accessible to the affected area) becomes numb and completely desensitized. You may feel a pins-and-needles sensation as an indication, or you can test the result by pinching the top of the hand with the non-anesthetized one. Then you can place the "glove" on the part of your body that is bothering you, thereby transferring the numbness to that area. The transference of insensitivity should last from four to eight hours. It is important that you remove the anesthesia from the "gloved" hand before coming out of trance, but that will not affect your pain control.

Note: In any pain control or healing techniques you should avoid using the word "pain" once you are communicating directly to the sub-

162

conscious. Remember the *Law of Dominant Effect*? Menti〔 something hurts you will likely emphasize the effect by dr〔 ᵤ mental energy to the word pain. I recommend that you use euphemisms such as "discomfort" or "that part that is bothering me".

As with all of the inductions in this book, someone can read this to you in a well-paced style with soft background music. Or, you can record the technique on tape for your personal use, but make sure to change the pronoun, "You" to "I", for the most effective results.

Begin by taking three to ten deep, cleansing breaths. With each intake you are increasing your body's natural healing ability. With each exhalation of breath you are releasing any of your attachments to your physical problem or discomfort. (At this point you can use your post-hypnotic cue or phrase to re-enter trance)

Now, as I count from one to five, with each number you feel so calm and so relaxed as if you had gone five long nights without sleep and with each number you are replacing a night of wonderful, restorative sleep. Just let yourself go. You are calm, tranquil and secure.

1 *Your breathing is deep, steady and relaxed. Your body temperature is normal, feeling neither warm nor cold. Your blood pressure is normal, neither high nor low. Comfortable, tranquil and secure from the top of your head, to the tips of your toes.*

2 *Noises or movements around you neither bother nor distract you. You remain focused on the sound of my voice, the pleasant music, and the wonderful sensations of relaxation spreading through your body.*

3 *So calm, so relaxed, from the top of your head to the tips of your toes. No problems or worries on your mind. What you are experiencing is a natural state of focused awareness. Let yourself go.*

4 *Thoughts about the past, or projects that you may have in the next few hours disappear temporarily from your mind, as you remain focused on the sound of my voice. The sensations are pleasant and this hypnotic rest is becoming more and more irresistible.*

5 *Deep sleep, deeper sleep, deepest sleep. Feeling so good, so calm, tranquil and relaxed.*

And now as I count from six to ten, you begin to feel so drowsy and so tired as if you had walked an incredible distance and all you want to do is rest and relax every muscle, nerve and bone in your body.

6 *Feel your eyelids now getting so heavy and so tired. So heavy and so tired as if they were slowly becoming glued tightly shut. Just let them relax and go deeper.*

7 *Feel your right arm and your left arm becoming so heavy and so tired as if each arm weighed about 75 lbs. It would take an extreme effort to lift them. So just let them relax and go deeper now.*

8 *Your whole body is feeling so heavy and so relaxed now, from the top of your head to the tips of your toes. Or perhaps you are feeling light and weightless with a pleasant tingling sensation. Just relax and let yourself go.*

9 *Feeling so good now. Calm, tranquil and relaxed. This is a natural state of focused awareness. You are completely in control in every moment of this exercise.*

10 *Deep sleep, deeper sleep, deepest sleep. Allow my voice to connect with your subconscious mind. You are calm, safe and secure within this peaceful state of hypnotic relaxation. No problems or worries on your mind.*

(A deepening procedure here is optional. If you feel sufficiently relaxed you may move on to the direct suggestion and imagery to produce glove anesthesia)

Imagine, if you will, that someone has just placed a large bucket filled with snow next to your (right/left) hand. The snow is pure and white and looks very inviting. It has a pleasant, fresh fragrance that reminds you of being in a winter wonderland. You gently slip your hand deep into the bucket and feel the delicious coolness enveloping your hand and wrist. The snow is cold, moist and fresh. You begin to feel a pleasant tingling sensation starting at the tip of your fingers and moving slowly up each finger, past the knuckle and into the space between each finger. The icy sensation is creeping up your hand, numbing the skin and penetrating deeply into the tissues. Although it seems like it has only been a brief instant since you first submerged your hand, many long minutes have passed. As the time passes by, your fingers and hand are becoming quite numb, so numb that it's as if you have received an injection of novocaine, like at the dentist. So numb that the skin and tissue are becoming impervious to any sensation. There is virtually no feeling in any part of your hand. It is icy cold. So cold, and numb and un-feeling.

You have had your hand immersed in that snow for many long minutes. Your hand has become icy cold and numb, as if it were anesthetized. I now invite you to remove your hand from the snow and place it on any part of your body that may be bothering you. As I count from one to four, you gently place that hand on any area of discomfort and you will transfer that lovely, icy, numbing sensation to that area. 1-2-3-4

Let it rest there now for just a few moments. And as it does, you feel that incredible numbing sensation transferring to that part of your body, completely removing any discomfort. How relieved you feel! And as you experience that transference, just let your hand drop by your side.

As your hand drops to your side you become more deeply relaxed. You are filled with a wonderful sense of well being. You appreciate the marvelous gifts of your mind and your capacity to produce glove anesthesia.

A warm breeze moves gently around your anesthetized hand, bringing the temperature back to normal. Your hand is recovering full sensation, blood is circulating throughout the veins and arteries. The skin and tissues of your hand are completely returning to their normal body temperature and sensation. Your hand feels warm, and normal, and relaxed. However, anytime that you wish to reproduce the phenomenon of glove anesthesia, all you have to do is re-enter your hypnotic trance by means of your post-hypnotic cue. Every time you enter trance you do so more rapidly and you go in more deeply. By suggesting the phrase, "icy cold hand", (you can replace this phrase with any word or cue that you choose) *within 15 seconds your hand becomes numb and insensitive and you are able to transfer that sensation to any body part that you desire. Glove anesthesia is easily reproduced when you tell yourself, "icy cold hand" once you are in the hypnotic state.*

As I count now from one to five, you will return to your normal, conscious state, feeling very alert and refreshed. Your hand is completely warm and back to normal circulation, and your affected body part remains nicely and comfortably numbed for many hours. 1-2-3-4-5. Wide awake now. Feeling wonderfully calm and alert

Healing and Pain Control

According to Chopra in *Ageless Body, Timeless Mind*, "the body is capable of producing any biochemical response once the mind has been given the appropriate suggestion."[37]   Through the mind/body connection you can alter sensations in your body, control pain, heal body parts and contour your muscles. In this section you will find additional techniques for pain control and some ideas of how to use your self-hypnosis to accelerate your recovery.

You should never rely solely on these methods when you have a physical problem or illness. Whether your preference is for traditional Western methods, or alternative care, I recommend that you first consult a professional. Once you have been given a diagnosis as well as advice by your health care professional you can then use self-hypnosis to participate more in the healing process. In the case of pain control, make sure that you use the techniques only in chronic situations— when you have already determined the source of the pain. If you have a sudden onset of pain, consult a physician to rule out any serious problem. When you have been advised by your health professional that there is nothing that can be done for you other than analgesics to alleviate the pain, then you can safely use these methods.

As mentioned in the previous section on "Glove Anesthesia", avoid using the word "pain" when you are communicating to the subconscious as this will likely emphasize the discomfort through the *Law of Dominant Effect*. Also, if you are working with chronic pain in an extremity, low back, or joint, be sure to leave a *signal pain*. This is a way of alerting you when you are over-stressing the area. You need to know when you are over-extending that shoulder area or bending down the wrong way and affecting your low back or you can cause further damage to the tissues.

For example, if you are doing pain control for a chronic ache in your right shoulder, make sure to add these words to your suggestion. Please note that the word pain never appears in the actual suggestion.

Because my shoulder is free of any discomfort, I am able to accomplish so much more. My movements are fluid and unimpeded, how-

167

ever, should I overextend or strain the muscles in my right shoulder in any way, I am immediately alerted by a signal of discomfort.

In the *Rules of Suggestion* one of the exceptions to stating all suggestions in present tense is in the case of healing a body part or illness. This is because the subconscious mind rules all of the bodily functions and if you tell it "My stomach is perfectly fine" it would reject that suggestion because it knows it to be untrue. Healing verbs should always be given in the present progressive tense, essentially adding the *"ing"*. Your subconscious has no problem with this, as it symbolizes process. In other words, "my stomach is healing and strengthening every day", is the proper way of phrasing suggestions of this nature. Holding a vision or image of the body part as completely healed and functioning optimally will enhance this suggestion.

It is a human tendency to seek pleasure and avoid pain. This is why we tend to automatically suppress issues—it is our way of not having to face or deal with the uncomfortable. These problems often wind up translating out to one of our organs, joints, or systems (circulatory, respiratory, digestive, etc.). The mind is equipped to deal with emotional issues, but the body is not. The end result is that the tissues deteriorate and become dis-eased. For this reason, stress is the major factor involved in almost all physical problems. That is why I emphasize the use of progressive relaxation as the foundation for *intentional states of hypnosis.*

When stress becomes localized in your elbow joint, your low back, or your colon, this is called a "focal point" or "hot spot". Chopra also states that every cell in our body is eavesdropping on our every thought. So when you say, "I can't stomach this situation any longer", or, "Having to deal with this is just killing me", you are giving literal instructions to your subconscious. And since stress creates the unintentional/subconscious dominant state, you are much more vulnerable to affecting your body adversely. Whenever you induce trance, make sure to pay particular attention to fully relaxing your hot spots. Some hot spots can be completely healed by facing what has been repressed in the subconscious and by releasing the stored feelings from the focal point.

168

Also, negative beliefs in the subconscious tend to generate negative emotions that have a toxic effect on the immune system and eventually bring about physical illness. By releasing those emotions in the various exercises offered in this section, you will create a much healthier physical condition.

The following induction can be used for all your self-hypnosis purposes, but it is especially effective for developing body consciousness. This technique is also ideal for those individuals who score high on "Kinesthetic" as it is easier for them to relate on a feeling level, rather than by visual imagery or direct suggestion. I recommend that you do this exercise lying down flat, preferably on the carpet. If you have any low back discomfort, place a pillow under your knees for support.

Somatic Induction

Let's start out by doing some deep breathing. Breathing is your fastest entry into your subconscious mind, as it turns your focus inward. Breathe in positive healing energy. Let that energy be a lovely pastel color. As you inhale, allow that soft color to permeate every cell and fiber of your being. As you exhale, allow any tensions, anxiety, discomfort or fear out through the soles of the feet. (At this point you can give yourself the Post-Hypnotic Suggestion to re-hypnotize).

Gently move your head from side to side, releasing any tension in your neck or the base of your skull. Then let it fall in a position that is the most comfortable. Allow it to rest and remain still in that position as you go deeper and deeper.

Now put your attention on the space in between your eyebrows, as if someone is pressing a button and you begin to squeeze your eyelids tightly shut. Squeeze them tighter and tighter. Stop squeezing now and allow all the hundreds of little muscles around your eyes just begin to grow loose, limp and relaxed. Now squeeze your entire face into a ball, making a funny face. As you release it, feel a wave of relaxation coming down every feature. You have the sensation that all of your features, all of the muscles on your face are melting, as you go deeper and deeper. It feels so good to let go.

169

Now squeeze your shoulders up to your ears, hold for a moment and squeeze tighter. Now just let go and release. If you tend to store tension in this area, perhaps do this one more time. It feels so good to deeply relax.

Focus your attention on your left hand, make a fist and squeeze tightly. Let it go and feel how the pressure drains away. Take your entire left arm and squeeze it against the ground or the bed. Lift your arm a few inches, let it fall and RELAX. Now repeat this on the right side. The greater the tension, the greater the release that follows.

In the entire middle part of your body, imagine that you have warm air circulating. Or maybe you'd find it more pleasant to imagine a cool breeze, however, don't squeeze this area. Now pull in your whole abdominal area as if a string were pulling it to the floor. Collapse your stomach. Now let go and relax. Deep sleep, deeper sleep, deepest sleep.

Now begin to wiggle your toes. Wiggle them faster and faster. Now stop the wiggling and just begin to move your toes in and out, flexing them inwards and outwards. Let them just fall to the side. Focus on your left foot. Flex it inwards, pointing the toes towards the ceiling. Squeeze and release. Point towards the opposite wall, hold and release. Now make a fist with your foot, squeeze it and let it go.

Push your entire left leg into the floor or bed. (Avoid this if you have lower back pain) *Now lift the leg a few inches off the floor and let it fall. Flex your right foot to the ceiling, squeeze and release. Point towards the opposite wall, hold and release. And now make a fist with your foot, squeeze it and let it go. Push your entire right leg into the floor or bed. Lift it a few inches off the floor and let it fall. Allow your entire body to rest and relax, going deeper with every breath.*

Pain Control I –The Switch Technique

Once you have entered the trance state, imagine yourself as being very tiny. Imagine that you are traveling down to the area at the base of your skull, where there is a control room, containing all the communication pathways to every nerve, muscle, organ and area of your body.

170

As you enter the control room you notice many flashing lights, but you are especially drawn to a flashing red light over a switch. This light is the area that is causing you discomfort. All of the nerves and muscles and tissues associated with the affected area can be accessed through this switch. The light is flashing to alert you that it is time to turn it off. See your hand reaching towards the switch—it is like a lever. Pull the lever down and as your hand leaves the switch you feel a tremendous relief washing over all of the muscles, nerves and tissues associated with the affected area. You feel so comfortable and relieved.

Pain Control II – The Sponge Technique

Imagine that someone who represents solace and nurturing is standing over you holding a giant sponge. This can be your mother as she appeared to you when you were a child, a guardian angel, a spouse or someone whose presence is comforting to you. Imagine that they are placing the sponge on the affected area. That sponge will soak up all of the discomfort and leave you relieved. Don't worry about anyone being contaminated by the sponge—it will be disposed of immediately and never bother anyone. Just make sure to let all of your discomfort be absorbed by the sponge. Now on the count of three, let it all go into the sponge. 1 - Let the sponge soak up the discomfort. 2 - Feel it all being drawn up and out of you by the sponge and 3 - Take a deep breath, let it go. You're feeling fine now.

Pain Control III – Altering Sensation

Once you have a detailed portrait, you can work within the trance to alter the sensation. Example: Ron described his migraine headaches as being sharp and throbbing. He envisioned them as dark gray spots that pulsed like a cement drill. In the hypnotic trance he simply manipulated the spots (both through imagery and suggestion) to become pale in color and to have a mild buzzing sound. He also modified the pain to be dull and pulsing. This was the first step to his overcoming these debilitating migraines. Eventually he succeeded in getting to the source of what was causing the headaches and they disappeared completely.

171

With this method you can also use suggestion and imagery to hallucinate sensations that would be soothing and easing to the pain. You can imagine an ice pack or a heating pad placed on the area. The phenomena associated with this suggestion will produce sensory changes. You can also imagine yourself in a Jacuzzi, sauna, ice drift, or any other symbol or image that suggests comfort.

Healing Suggestion

Each day the healing powers of my creative intelligence are healing, strengthening, and making my _____ healthier than ever. This tremendously accelerated healing process is occurring in me right now.

Healing I – The Rays of the Sun

Imagine yourself lying on a beach or in a flower-filled meadow. This is mid-day and the ground has already been warmed by hours of sunlight. You feel the warmth permeating into your back muscles and all along your spine, causing you to relax more deeply into the ground or sand. The rays of the sun are very beneficial to you. You feel all of the muscles of your scalp, forehead, face muscles, ears and throat completely melt and relax. The sunlight warms all of the organs of your body. You feel the gentle rays warming your abdomen, hips, thighs and feet, all the way down to your toes. Now mentally move those sun rays up to the part of your body that needs healing. Concentrate all of the sun's energy on that part. The light of the sun is a prism of gorgeous pastel colors that are all focused on healing you. Allow yourself to be healed. Create a vision of that body part as completely healed and functioning optimally.

Healing II – Dialoguing with the Non-Dominant Hand

Lucia Capacchione has found an incredible way of communicating with the subconscious.[39] She pioneered the concept of carrying on a dialogue through the interaction of both hands, forming questions with the dominant hand and answering with the non-dominant. Her theory is that our dominant hand represents the left hemisphere of the brain, which functions more chronologically and logically. The non-dominant hand is our link to the right hemisphere, associated more with creativity and spatial perceptions. By using this method we can often access symbolic messages from the subconscious. I was fortunate enough to attend a workshop on this technique in the early 80's and have discovered a lot of revelations through my left (non-dominant) hand.

This is actually very easy. Let's say you are right-handed and have chronic gastritis. Take a piece of paper and two different colored pens. You will ask questions and make comments with your dominant (in this case, right) hand. The answers will come from the non-dominant hand (in this case, left). Starting out with the right hand you will write: *Question: Why is my stomach feeling this way?* Then pick up the other pen with your left hand and begin writing. It may feel weird at first, but just go with it. Don't worry about grammar, spelling, penmanship or syntax. No on else will be looking at this. So, for instance, the left may answer: *You are ignoring my requests for more down time.* Then carry on a dialogue, with the right hand asking what it can specifically do to remedy the situation. By utilizing this method you can bring a lot of consciousness to otherwise unknown aspects of your psyche.

Creating Your Safe Haven

Everyone needs some personal space—in the outer world, as well as the inner. Even if the time limitations and logistics of a busy life do not provide as much physical space as you might like, you can always go into your subjective world and enjoy some private time.

Safe place imagery is one of the most versatile applications of the altered state. Within the secluded world that you create you can accomplish an amazing variety of healing at the subconscious level. This technique also makes unpleasant situations and tedious periods more bearable, such as having dental work or enduring long plane trips. From 1994 to 1996 I was traveling virtually every month to Japan—a 12-hour flight and then an additional two hours by bus to get into Tokyo. There are only so many books and magazines you can read or movies you can watch without getting serious cabin fever on such a long flight. By means of self-hypnosis, I particularly love to transport myself to my favorite spots on the planet, such as the Columbia River Gorge on the Oregon-Washington border, where I envision myself floating on a raft. It makes for a nice diversion. Here are some ideas for utilizing your safe haven:

• If you are having a medical or dental procedure, simply close your eyes, do some deep breathing and transport yourself to your safe haven by means of a post-hypnotic suggestion. This is referred to as *dissociation*. Taking such a pleasurable trip without the assistance of any drugs is a great diversion when you are having cavities drilled or a pap smear.

• Let's say you have a presentation to give at work or need to address a group and public speaking has never been your forte. Rehearse your lines in the security of your haven several times. By training your subconscious to carry an image of you successfully getting your point across, this will build up your self-confidence. You can also use a post-hypnotic suggestion directly before the speaking engagement, so that your subconscious smoothly takes over. This will help you bypass the critical factor of the mind, which tends to make you self-conscious. (See the preceding section on "Post-Hypnotics")

• In the sanctuary of your haven, you can work through emotional issues with people that you are having problems with. Simply invite them to be present on an energetic level and express how you feel to them. This is a much healthier way of venting hurt and anger before actually having a meeting face to face where you run the risk of intensifying the disagreement. Within your safe haven you are naturally in control and can say anything that you'd like, however, do allow some time for rebuttal on their part. This may only seem like an imaginary game, but you might "hear" something that can get you to reflect more deeply.

• You may also invite into your sanctuary those individuals who are no longer on the planet, such as deceased relatives or mentors. Although they are not present in a physical sense, there is always an energetic imprint of each person that has touched your life within your subconscious landscape. When someone passes away we might feel abandoned or frustrated because we have not been able to express our true feelings. Maybe we would like to seek forgiveness or we are ready to let go of non-productive emotions. I worked this way with my mother who died at 58 of cancer. This was helpful in working through old resentments that I knew were holding me back from my emotional and spiritual growth. You can also invite individuals that you've never met, yet have impacted your life in an inspirational way. There is a technique in Napoleon Hill's *Think and Grow Rich* which suggests that you have a round table conference with any innovative or enlightened being that can offer you motivation and wisdom and help you to brainstorm on new projects.[40] For instance, you can share some quality time with Jesus Christ, Buddha, Thomas Edison, Shakespeare, or Mother Theresa—anyone that you consider a source of illumination! I have spent some enlightening moments in my safe haven with Carl Gustav Jung, the brilliant psychoanalyst and philosopher.

• Use this special place to deal with any fears that you may be harboring. Fears can either be experiential (you were bit by a dog and now you are afraid of them) or irrational (you have no conscious knowledge as to why you might fear something like snakes, heights, or elevators). Either way, they are definitely controlling your mind and body. Regression work is probably the most effective way to deal with fears, but this technique will also eliminate many of them effortlessly.

A behavior modification technique called *systematic desensitization*, created by Wolpe, trained patients to relax all of the major muscle groups and imagine as vividly as possible the anxiety-provoking items, stopping immediately when they began to feel anxious. Then they were asked to repeat the process for longer and longer periods until they could maintain the state of relaxation[41]. You can face your fears in this secure environment as a way of rehearsing your reactions and desensitizing your anxiety. Also, because this is a world created solely by your imagination, you can manipulate the image in any way to make it less threatening. For instance, make a rat a furry pet that wants to play with you and is totally non-threatening. Fade images, expand or contract them, according to your needs.

• Feel free to invite any non-physical entities into your realm. For instance, if you resonate with angels, ask that your guardian angel be present in any of the work that you do in your safe haven. *Angel Blessings* has been an incredible inspiration for me and many of my friends over the years: You are introduced to 44 exquisite angel cards and an accompanying workbook outlining special exercises and meditations related to each of their specific duties, such as *Shushienae,* Angel of Purity and *Raphael*, the Archangel of Healing.[42] They will be delighted to be summoned into your haven.

Begin now by closing your eyes and allowing your body to relax. As you breathe in, your body fills with peace and tranquility. And as you exhale, let any of the tensions or pressures you may have been holding in your body escape through the soles of your feet. I'd like you now to imagine that you are at the top of a winding staircase that has ten wide steps. And as I count from ten to one I would like for you to descend one step at a time, with each step deepening your relaxation (or hypnotic trance) 100 times. When you reach the last step you will find yourself 1,000 times more relaxed, calm, and peaceful.

Starting now with the number ten, take your first step. You feel very secure and protected. Your subconscious mind is connected with my voice.

9   Going deeper now. Very peaceful. Let yourself go 100 times deeper.

8   Feeling so relaxed. Allowing every nerve and muscle in your body to relax.

7   This hypnotic relaxation is so pleasant for you. You let go of any thoughts about the past or preoccupation about the future and find yourself completely tranquil within the present moment.

6   Your breathing remains so deep and steady. Let yourself go.

5   Halfway there now. 500 times more relaxed. So calm, tranquil and serene.

4   You wouldn't trade this wonderful feeling for anything in the world because as you enter into your inner world you are experiencing complete peace and serenity.

3   Going deeper now. Very calm, from the top of your head to the tip of your toes.

2   Your mind is free of any tensions, yet very alert and connected to my voice.

1   1,000 times deeper. Let yourself go. So calm, tranquil and re-laxed.

You find yourself now in a hallway. Walking down the corridor you encounter a door with your name written on it in bronze letters. When you open the door you enter a multi-media room, the kind found in television studios, where there is an editing console and a wall with nine television screens. On each of the screens is a very pleasant scene. Please sit down at the console. Before you are knobs and buttons that I invite you to operate. As you do, the images on the screens will change. When you find a particularly pleasing scene, let it rest there. Perhaps one will be an exotic waterfall, or a sandy beach. One may be a comfortable sofa placed in front of a warm and inviting fireplace. Allow your imagination to be projected onto the screens because you are creating a haven for the inner work that you are embarking upon. This haven may be indoors or outdoors, or a combination of both. Or if you prefer, the nine screens may represent different feelings and qualities that you desire to take with you into your safe haven. Take a few moments now to construct your special place, one that will inspire and protect you on your journey to self-realization.

When you have all nine screens displaying your chosen scenes or feelings, look to the right of you on the console. You will find a large blue button. Press that button now. The wall with the screens is rising up, retracting into the ceiling and before you is your safe haven! I invite you now to enter into this realm. As you leave the studio behind, the wall will come back into place and you find yourself in this idyllic setting which you have created. If you are indoors, I would like you to consciously seal the building or structure from any unwanted influences. You might want to imagine a white light with golden sparkles at the periphery of your realm. If you are in an outdoor setting you may want to enclose this inner world with a bubble or a rainbow of protection and security. You are completely safe within this realm. All of the work done here is dynamic and life-affirming and you have the power to banish any force or emotion that is threatening to you. You may imagine yourself in a dialogue or interaction with anyone in your world, however, you are immune to any manipulation or stress. Here you are totally protected. Take a few moments to appreciate the beautiful space that you have created.

Encounter with Innocence

As children we had a natural innocence. We were born free of prejudices and hate, wanting to love and be loved. Somewhere along the way we suffered wounds and these left imprints on our subconscious minds, which were then reproduced as holographic images within the mind field. The build-up of painful images, feelings, and messages trapped in our energetic field constantly bombarded us to the point that we began to shut down, losing the joy, innocence and spontaneity of childhood. The child we were at every wounding experienced in our young lives remains as a virtual hologram within the subconscious. Desperately lonely, yet terrified of being vulnerable, these inner children haunt us and sabotage our close relationships. They don't mean us any harm – this is their way of imploring us to take notice. Once you acknowledge the existence of your inner child tremendous shifts will take place in your life.

In reality we cannot go back to our childhood and demand that our parents give us the upbringing that we would have liked. We cannot rationally depend on anyone outside of ourselves to take over the parent role once we are adults. This would only weaken us and create co-dependence. But *you* can re-parent your inner child and offer him or her the security of your unconditional love and acceptance. Researchers have found that the unconditional support and love of one parent figure in a child's life is enough to create emotional well-being. It's not too late for you to function as that nurturing parent. A secure child is one who plays and learns with equal intensity. An emotionally healthy child expresses love and joy and allows for intimacy in relationships. This is the Divine Child that Carl Gustav Jung described as our golden potential for self-realization.[43]

In this exercise, you will remember a time when you were hurt as a child, allowing the full force of any emotions that you may have repressed to flow unimpeded. If you have experienced something that you know to be extremely traumatic, such as being sexually molested, or losing a parent, you may choose to do this work with a therapist present, so that they can safely guide you through without danger of becoming engulfed by the sentiment. Or choose an event that, while painful, is something that you will not be overwhelmed by reliving. You will then reconnect with the child who was left behind and offer them an opportunity to tell their story. Then by gaining the confidence of your inner child, he or she can integrate into your consciousness, allowing for what poet Lawrence Ferlinghetti describes as a *renaissance of wonder.*[44]

Sometimes the child that you encounter in this exercise may be distant or reluctant to communicate with you. Don't allow this to discourage you. There are deep trust issues here that need to be resolved. Your inner child might need some assurances that he or she will not soon be abandoned again. He or she may be hurt that they have been neglected for so long. Let them know that you are giving them the space to be authentic in their feelings. If you care enough to journey back to the meeting place, you will find the inner child increasingly more receptive. Be patient. The rewards are many!

Meeting Your Inner Child

As you breathe deeply, imagine yourself protected by a beautiful white light with golden sparkles. This is the light of security and protection, light that comes from the Divine. Breathe in the safety of that light. As you breathe out, willingly let go of any of those dark areas inside of you. Release any attachments to those dark areas. Let yourself go more with each and every breath. (At this point use your post-hypnotic suggestion to re-enter trance. While an induction is optional, you will increase your comfort and receptivity by practicing a progressive relaxation)

And now, in the hypnotic state, your imagination becomes very real to you. You feel yourself moving back through time and space to an event in your life that was quite sad. Something that happened when you were a child, that makes you feel hurt and may have caused you to weep. Be aware of any sights, sounds, or feelings connected to the experience. Were there any smells or tastes associated with this moment? You may relive this experience through all of your five senses as if it were the first time. Or you may choose to see it as if you were watching a big screen television with the remote in hand. You can adjust the picture or sound: you can make the images smaller, or even turn the power switch "off" if at any time it becomes too painful to you. Or, you may just recall an experience vaguely—in this case, pay attention to your emotions and any sensations that may be coming up in your body. Get a sense of the child you were then. How old were you? How were you dressed? What were you doing?

Feel the emotion well up inside your chest cavity. Allow any tears that come into your eyes to flow. Remember how very sad this experience was and how much it hurt your feelings.

Now it's time to release those feelings. Let them all come up from out of your heart, out of your chest, out of your mind, your throat, your diaphragm, or any other place in your body that you may be storing them. Imagine or visualize them rising up and being caught in a net way above you. All of those sad and hurt feelings are gathered into that net and are being funneled into a container. See or imagine that container in your mind. See or imagine it being filled up with those

181

sad and hurt feelings that you have released. You may feel yourself becoming lighter. You may experience a drop-off of energy or sense of exhaustion. Just keep letting those feelings rise up and be funneled into the container.

Now imagine that you are holding a blowtorch. See, feel, or hear yourself igniting that torch and aiming it right at the container. Shoot a brilliant white flame at the container until it is engulfed by the light. The white light is transmuting all of the feelings trapped in the container. They are being purified and released into the atmosphere as totally harmless atoms of energy. Let them float off and disappear. Very good – you're doing so well. Just rest and relax a few moments. Let go of the past. You are just here in the moment enjoying deep relaxation and inner peace.

See yourself now as the adult that you are, in this present time, walking in a park in the early morning. You are the first one there and enjoying the solitude, the quiet, and the peace. The sky has re-markable colors in the early dawn. There are birds calling to one another. The dew is still fresh on the grass and flowers. There are a multitude of sights, sounds, and smells. You feel the soft breeze against your face as you walk through this park.

In the near distance is a bank of trees. You walk toward the trees, fully enjoying this solitary time in nature. As you approach the trees, you notice a young child sitting with his/her back towards you. Con-cerned, you walk toward the child to find out if everything is okay. As the child turns towards you, you are looking at yourself (at the age when you were wounded), looking very sad. This child has been hurt. This child is not sure of his/her self-worth or importance here on the planet. However, you are the ideal person to help heal and guide this child into their full potential. Are you willing to do this work? Good. Then in the following silence you are connecting to and communicat-ing with your inner child. Let him/her tell their story. Or maybe your child just wants to play with you or feel your presence. (Pause for several minutes)

Before you leave your inner child, make some kind of agreement with him or her as to what activities you can do in your daily life that

182

will bring them closer to you or allow them to feel safer. Perhaps you may want to go into this park from time to time so you can meet and play together. Coming up now with a beautiful sense of well being at the count of five. Feeling joyful and innocent and very much at peace with yourself.

1-2-3-4-5

I will share my recommendation to all of my age regression clients and students over the years: within a few days of completing this exercise you may want to visit a toy store or novelty shop and look for a toy, doll, figurine or stuffed animal that somehow represents the essence of your inner child. You will have an immediate sense of recognition when you have spotted the right object. By having this doll or toy in a conspicuous place—perhaps where you can see it upon going to sleep at night or waking up in the morning—it tends to communicate a message to your subconscious that you are taking the responsibility to nurture yourself.

A few years ago while doing an inner child process, my little seven-year-old Linda told me that she wanted to see zebras. My first zebra was a paper towel dispenser that a therapist friend gave me when I shared the story. The zebras started piling up once I got the word out and started collecting: art work, figurines, beanie babies, kitchenware and T-shirts! It was not a coincidence that a tremendous amount of healing took place over the next few months. Find out what your inner child might like as a token or symbol of your commitment to self-love.

Scripts

These are sample self-hypnosis scripts for five of the most universal themes that come up in my classes. Feel free to use them or make modifications, but I hope that you will make the effort to personalize them, beginning with the worksheet recommended in your *Tool Kit.* I cannot over-emphasize the importance of tailoring suggestion to your personal needs. In this way you can more effectively target the "first thoughts" and intentions behind negative thinking and behavior patterns in order to make a permanent change.

Stopping Smoking

I am a successful non-smoker. I feel myself walking through a world of vitality, health, and personal power. I own my body. I own my mind. I have free will and choose vitality, health, and personal power. There are so many new pleasures in my life. I feel so good about myself that I am a non-smoker.

I am finding so many wonderful ways to nurture myself. There is no substitute for self-love and personal power. At any time that I feel any urge, or craving, or desire not congruent with my personal power, I take three deep breaths. Those deep inhalations of fresh air and oxygen fill my lungs, and any cravings instantly disappear.

My taste buds savor so many more exquisite flavors, my sense of smell allows for so many more delights, because I am a successful non-smoker. My breath is clean, my hair, clothes, and environment are clean and fresh. Just as I have reached other positive goals in my life, I have accomplished becoming a non-smoker. I have so many more positive goals before me. They are all attainable because of my tremendous vitality, health, and personal power. Every area of my life is improving. I am a winner.

Letting Go of the Past

I agree to be fully present now in my heart, mind, and emotions. I choose to fully occupy my space and time to accomplish my mission here on earth and to live freely and joyfully. I accept that I cannot change what has happened in the past and I gladly release any emotions that are holding me back from expressing my full potential. I forgive myself and others because I realize that anything that has occurred has ultimately served me in a positive way. Letting go of the past is a creative and proactive choice and I am proud of myself for making it.

In fact, the past now seems like old movies and soap operas, which are a part of my history. That history has no power over my mental images, no power over my self-esteem, nor any power over my relationships. As I count from ten to one, my bonds to the past are dissolving. It is my history, but can no longer affect my present condition. 10-9-8-7-6-5-4-3-2-1. The past is dissolving. I am free. I feel as if a tremendous weight has lifted from my shoulders. I feel a release in my heart, in my mind, and in my emotions.

Throughout the day I am aware of this pleasant lightness in my heart, mind and emotions. I am free. I fully occupy this time and space to accomplish more and more every day. I have learned the lessons from the past and am now applying them to a more satisfying present and an extraordinary future. My life is a clean slate, full of light and potential. I am a loving person with peace in my mind and my heart. Everything is possible now.

Releasing Anger

I now choose to release any negative emotions that I have been carrying towards myself or others. These feelings no longer serve me for my highest good. I am an emotionally mature individual, capable of handling all issues and relationships with tolerance and understanding. I am open to communication and others admire me for my tolerance and patience. There is nothing in the past that can interfere with my commitment to live harmoniously with others. From this day forward I break the hold that negative emotions have had on my life. I am in complete control of my emotions at all times.

At any time that I experience a build-up of negative emotions, I

185

easily release them by taking several deep breaths. All negative emotions are effortlessly discharged through my exhalation. I visualize or imagine that these non-productive energies are funneled into a container and taken far away where they harm no one. It is easy for me to let go of negative emotions.

I am free of the toxicity of negative emotions. My brain is operating more effectively. I have more personal power. My health is improving. I radiate well-being mentally, physically, and spiritually. My life is becoming incredibly peaceful and I am free to accomplish so much more. I enjoy relating to others. My friends and family members are delighted by the changes in me. I am admired by others for my tolerance and patience. I have broken the chains of negative emotions and welcome peace into my world. I handle all of life's challenges with tolerance and understanding. Solutions come effortlessly to me with my expanded brain-power. How wonderful it feels to accept myself and others.

Inspiring Faith

I believe that the Universe is on my side. I believe in a Creator who is looking out for my best interests and holds a vision of my highest potential. I surrender to a Higher Will, fully aware that I am safe and protected at all times. From this day forward every aspect of my life and personality is improving because I have faith. Faith is knowing that there is a light at the end of the tunnel. Faith is trusting that when one door closes, another will open. Faith is awakening to the knowledge that I am here for a purpose and I am continually filled with hope. Faith assures me that I am on the right path. I understand now that all of my suffering has served to teach and strengthen me and I release any fear or pain that might be holding me back. At this very moment, I let go of any of my attachments or expectations because I have faith that my life is unfolding perfectly. I no longer have any need to control the outcome, because I have faith that I am protected at all times.

I welcome any guidance and inspiration from my Superconscious mind. I understand that I am not alone on this path and I am open to receiving hunches and intuition. These are messages to guide me and assist me. I am awakening to the knowledge that I am protected at all times. How wonderful to know that everything in my life has meaning. I plan now with faith and confidence because I was born with a special mission and I am here to excel. I believe in myself. This unshakable, unbreakable faith causes me to laugh and smile more than 200 times every day. Life is pleasant and holds so many opportunities. Life is offering me new delights every day because of my faith. My faith increases every day and cannot be altered by criticism, comments or problems. I am guided and protected at all times.

Self-Confidence

From this day forward my positive self-confidence transforms any situation. I have the courage to face any of life's challenges. I am a worthwhile individual with much to offer the world. I know that anything that I may have experienced in the past has only served to test me and strengthen me. My self-confidence and determination easily neutralize any of the negative ghosts of the past. Those old scripts, feelings, and images have no power over my emotions. Nor do they have any influence over my reactions and choices. I am free to choose anything that I desire, providing that it is harmless to myself and others. My positive determination magnetizes and draws to me all that I set forth to accomplish.

I spend at least five minutes several times a day practicing conscious breathing. This fully oxygenates my brain and activates my vast potential. Deep breathing links my conscious and subconscious minds and creates full cooperation between the multiple dimensions of my being. As I am fully present, I am capable of extraordinary stamina, increased will power, and greater memory, concentration and logic.

My communication skills are improving. All comments and criticisms directed towards me are interpreted as constructive advice to assist me in being the best that I can be. People are attracted and charmed by my charisma and good will. As a self-confident individual I am a positive force for good on this planet. I am a brilliant example

187

of expanded human potential. My self-confidence is like a waterfall, cascading over every cell and fiber of my body, rejuvenating each and every organ and system. I am bold, perseverant, optimistic and aggressive. Every day life is providing unlimited opportunities to me.

Conclusion

In this manual my objective was to give you an overview of the power of thought and a way to have some control over the experiences that your mind may be generating unconsciously. Yet I am very much aware that there is exhaustive research being conducted at major universities on the mind and the brain. You may have noticed that I have treated the mind as a kind of abstract concept, with very little reference to the brain and its complex wiring. I believe that studying some of the papers and books outlining the advances in neuroscience would be a better source for the reader to understand more of the intricacies of the human brain and the elaboration of experience into concrete thought. Through my own research I have found much to concur with some of my ideas and theories. I have deliberately bypassed the more technica information with the intention of having the reader identify and focus ore on one's personal experience of reality.

I would also like to emphasize that the concepts in this book are not meant to interfere with any of the reader's personal values or beliefs. There was no agenda to create any kind of spiritual philosophy or creed. I believe that the information, exercises, and techniques presented in *The Owner's Manual* can enhance one's personal relationship to whatever Higher Power one worships. There is also no assumption that you must believe in a higher power in order to achieve significant results from the material presented here. The more you free yourself of feelings of guilt, unworthiness, stagnation, and resentment, the more open you can become to the notion that we live in a benevolent universe that allows us the freedom of choice and personal creativity.

There is so much practical wisdom in the phrase *"if you don't go within, you go without"*.[45] There is no longer any reason for you to be going *without* in your life. There is no longer any reason for you to be missing out on a reality that is considerably more bliss than woe. This manual has been an invitation to go within and to understand the forces that have formed your present reality. Embarking on the journey to explore the realm of the subconscious is one that takes much courage. Even if you aren't aware of being courageous, your subconsciouscarries that positive trait as well as many others. Explore the inner world of your mind and you will discover endless treasures.

For information regarding seminars, workshops, consultations, cassettes, or aromatherapy essential oils, you may contact the author directly:

Linda Joy Rose, Ph.D.
351 N. Newport Blvd. Suite 528
Newport Beach, CA 92663
www.drlindarose.com

To subscribe to my free monthly self-help newsletter or for any inquireies, send an email to:

feedback@drlindarose.com

Glossary

Abreaction   Emotional response to repressed material arising from the subconscious mind.

Affirmation   A statement of universal truth that can serve as a positive suggestion to motivate the subconscious.

Alpha   Brain wave pattern associated with a light trance state.

Amnesia   The loss of memory. The amnesia that occurs in hypnosis may be either spontaneous or induced by suggestion, but is never permanent.

Autonomic Nervous System A part of the peripheral nervous system regulating involuntary responses, especially those concerned with survival, nutritive, vascular, and productive activities.

Beta   Brain wave pattern associated with the waking, conscious state.

Catalepsy   Muscular rigidity connected with the extremities. The medium level of hypnosis.

Critical Factor   The protective filter separating the conscious and subconscious minds.

Delta   Brain wave pattern associated with dreamless sleep. Delta waves have also been found in hypnotic subjects experiencing regressions to childhood and past lives.

Fight or Flight response The activation of the survival response in the limbic system. An inherited trait from primitive mind.

Glove Anesthesia   Producing a loss of sensation in one hand which can then be transferred to another body part as a means of numbing or alleviating pain.

Healing Crisis   Stage following emotional release from the subconscious in which feelings may be intensified and uncomfortable.

191

Hypermnesia	Enhanced memory. One of the hypnotic phenomena, it is useful for exploring the subconscious identifications.
Hypnotic phenomena	Exceptional characteristics of the subconscious mind which are activated via suggestion in the hypnotic state.
Identification	The internal elaboration of experience. A subjective perception of a past event.
Induction	Method for deliberately guiding one into an altered state of consciousness.
Intentional Hypnosis	A deliberate usage of the trance state, either self-directed or guided by a therapist or audio-cassette.
Law of Concentrated Attention	Whenever your attention is focused on an idea, that idea tends to realize itself.
Law of Dominant Effect	The suggestion presented to the mind carrying the most powerful emotion will displace any other suggestion in the mind at the time.
Law of Reversed Effect	The harder you try to do something, the less you are able to do it.
Mind Field	The portion of the Human Energy Field that contains our innermost thoughts, feelings, and images. The Mind Field works as a radar that picks up signals from the outside world, as well.
Post-Hypnotic Suggestion	Suggestions given in the trance or hypnotic state, intended for the subconscious to act upon and carry out in the normal, waking state.
Primitive Mind	A deeper layer of the subconscious mind, in which we are pre-programmed with certain instincts an impulses. Similar to Jung's "collective unconscious".
Programming	The early subconscious input that determines one's belief systems, attitudes, feelings, thoughts, and actions.
Progressive Relaxation	A systematic easing of all the major muscle groups with the intention of reducing stress or entering into an altered state of consciousness.

Stage Hypnosis	Hypnosis for entertainment purposes.
Subconscious	The portion of the mind or mental operation below the level of conscious awareness. The place where one's programming is stored. The seat of our imagination and emotions.
Suggestion	A word, group of words, images, phrases, ideas or concepts that instructs the subconscious to reorganize its thoughts or actions.
Superconscious	The highest and most noble aspect of mind, containing the seeds of one's mission or destiny.
Theta	Brain wave pattern associated with the dream stage of sleep and of medium to deep trance levels.
Time distortion	One of the hypnotic phenomena – a mental manipulation of the concept of linear time where it can appear to be either expanded or contracted.
Trance	The altered state of consciousness, profound abstraction or being hypnotized.
Unintentional Hypnosis	Natural state that occurs when the subconscious becomes dominant and is then open to suggestion. Certain factors such as extreme anxiety or shock can also produce this state.

References

1. Ferrucci, Piero, *What We May Be,* Jeremy P. Tarcher, Inc., New York, NY 1982

2. Tebbetts, Charles, *Self Hypnotis and Other Mind Expanding Techniques,* Westwood Publishing, Los Angeles, CA 1977

3. Bradshaw, John, *Bradshaw On: The Family,* Health Communica-tions, Deerfield Beach, FL, 1988

4 Preston, Michael, Ph.D., "Why Hypnosis Works", *Medical Hypnoanalysis Journal,* September 1989

5. Helmstetter, Shad, Ph.D., *What to Say When You Talk to Yourself,* Simon & Schuster, New York, NY 1982

6. LeCron, Leslie, *Hypnotism Today,* Wilshire Books, North Hollywood, CA 1947.

7. Krasner, A.M., Ph.D., *The Wizard Within,* American Board of Hypnotherapy Press, Santa Ana, CA 1991

8. Gawain, Shakti, *Creative Visualization,* New World Library, San Rafael, CA, Rev. Ed. 1995

9. Gawain, 1995

10. Russell, Paul, "How Ideas Bend the World into Shape", *Foundations of Consciousness,* 1997

11. Walsch, Neale Donald, *Conversations with God, Book I,* G.P. Putnam & Sons, New York, NY, 1995

12. Dossey, Larry, *Be Careful What You Pray For…You Just May Get It,* Harper San Francisco, San Francisco, CA 1997

13. Zukav, Gary, *The Seat of the Soul,* Simon & Schuster, New York, NY, 1989

14. Gerber, Richard, *Vibrational Medicine,* Bear & Co., Santa Fe, NM, 1988

15. Talbot, Michael, *The Holographic Universe,* Harper Perennial, New York, NY, 1991

16. Myss, Caroline, *Anatomy of a Spirit,* Three Rivers Press, New York, NY, 1996

17. Chopra, Deepak, *The Seven Spiritual Laws of Success,* Amber-Allen Publishing and New World Library, San Rafael, CA, 1993

18. Shinn, Florence Scovel, *The Game of Life and How to Play It,* Fireside, Simon & Schuster, New York, NY, 1925

19. Virtue, Doreen, *Angel Therapy,* Hay House, Inc., Carlsbad, CA, 1997

20. Zukav, 1989

21. Borysenko, Joan, Ph.D., *Fire in the Soul,* Warner Books, New York, NY, 1993

22. Frankl, Viktor, *Man's Search for Meaning,*
    Simon & Schuster, New York, NY, 1959, 1984

23. Williamson, Marianne, *A Return to Love,* HarperCollins, New York, NY, 1992.

24. Bradshaw, 1988

25. Rossi, Ernest Lawrence, Ph.D., *The 20 Minute Break: Using the New Science of Ultradian Rhythms,* Jeremy P. Tarcher, Inc., Los Angeles, CA, 1991

26. Paramahansa Yogananda, *Autobiography of a Yogi,*
    Self-Realization Fellowship, Los Angeles, CA, 1946, 1990

27. Govindan, M., M.A., *Babaji and the 18 Siddha Kriya Yoga Tradition,*
    Kriya Yoga Publications, Montreal, Canada, 1991

28. Harre, Rom & Lamb, Roger, *The Encyclopedic Dictionary of Psychology,*
    The MIT Press, Cambridge, MA, 19983

29. Krasner, 1991

30. Peck, M. Scott, *The Road Less Traveled,*

31. Gawain, 1995

32. Covey, Stephen R., *The 7 Habits of Highly Effective People,*
    Fireside Simon & Schuster, New York, NY 1989

33. Temple, Robert, *Open to Suggestion: The Uses and Abuses of Hypnosis,*
    The Aquarian Press, Northampshire, England, 1989

34. Weil, Andrew M.D., *8 Weeks to Optimum Health,*
    Fawcette Ballantine, New York, NY, 1997

35. Worwood, Valerie, *The Fragrant Mind,* New World Library, Novato, CA, 1996

36. Hay, Louise, *You Can Heal Your Life,*
    Hay House, Inc., Santa Monica, CA, 1984

37. Chopra, Deepak, *Ageless Body, Timeless Mind,*
    Harmony Books,   New York, NY 1993.

38. *Handbook of Hypnotic Suggestions and Metaphors*

39. Capacchione, Lucia, M.A., *The Power of Your Other Hand*, Newcastle Publishing Co., Inc., North Hollywood, CA, 1988

40. Hill, Napoleon, *Think & Grow Rich*, Fawcett Crest, New York, NY, 1960

41. Hall, Calvin S. & Lindzey, Gardner, *Theories of Personality*, 3rd Ed., Wiley & Sons, New York, NY, 1978

42. Marooney, Kimberly, *Angel Blessings: Cards of Sacred Guidance & Inspiration*, Merrill-West Publishing, Carmel, CA, 1995

43. Jung, Carl Gustav, *The Collected Works, Vol. 9.i*, 3rd Printing, Princeton Press, Princeton, NJ, 1950

44. Ferlinghetti, Lawrence, "I Am Waiting", *A Coney Island of the Mind*

45. Walsch, 1995

ORDER YOUR COMPANION TAPE SERIES

You can activate the power of your subconscious mind through these pre-recorded audio-cassettes featuring the soothing and professional hypnotic voice of Dr. Linda Joy Rose. These tapes are enhanced by original music that utilizes alpha and theta brain waves to guide you into a deep state of relaxation.

Each tape has **a separate technique on each side** and costs only $12.00. You can purchase the set of three tapes, with six of the most important exercises featured in this book, for only $30.00 (you save $6.00). By 2005 these will be available on audio CD format.

Please indicate which tape(s) you are ordering. Enclose a check or money order payable to Linda Joy Rose, Ph.D. and include shipping and handling amount as shown on the order form next page. California residents add 7.75% tax. For credit card orders (MC, Visa, American Express) please write your card number and expiration date. All payments must be in US funds.

OM-1 Side A - Hypnotic Programming
(Prepares you to enter the hypnotic state with induction, deepening techniques, relaxation, and cues to re-hypnotize easily)

Side B - Glove Anesthesia
(Pain control through the power of your mind)

OM-2 Side A - The Garden of Beliefs
(Re-discover your unique gifts, life purpose, and mission for this lifetime)

Side B - Creating Your Safe Haven
(Create a space of pure safety where you are free to explore your potential)

OM-3 Side A - Reprogramming the Data Base
(An indispensable technique for letting go of your outdated belief programs and non-productive emotional data)

Side B - Discovering Your First Thought
(A vital exercise for uncovering the root of what may be blocking you from achieving success)

A Year of Positive Habits – The workbook that will change your life!
Dr. Rose's new workbook guides you through a fun and realistic twelve-stage self-improvement program to boost your self-esteem, productivity and the overall quality of your life. **$19.95**

Parallel Lives: Exploring your quantum selves
Dr. Rose's original modality based on the quantum mechanics concept of simultaneous time. Exciting guidelines for reviewing and recreating your significant life choices. Workbook format. **$14.95**

Allow 3-4 weeks for delivery.
Please use (or copy) the Order Form on next page

For more information, call: 1-866-983-2479
Or fax: (949) 481-3147
Or email at: feedback@drlindarose.com

Order Form

OM-1   Qty. _____ x $12.00 =   _____

OM-2   Qty. _____ x $12.00 =   _____

OM-3   Qty. _____ x $12.00 =   _____

3-Tape Set   Qty. _____ x $30.00 =   _____

A Year of ... Qty. _____ x $19.95 =   _____

Parallel Lives Qty. _____ x $14.95 =   _____

Shipping & Handling to:
US   orders below $30.00 $2.00
US   orders above $30.00 $3.50

Canada and overseas orders below $30.00 $4.00
Canada and overseas orders above $30.00 $8.00

                                    s/h: _____

California residents add 7.75% sales tax: _____

                          Total: _____

Name: _____

Address: _____

City: _____ State or Prov. _____

Country: _____ Zip or postal code : _____

Telephone with area/country code: _____

Email address: _____

  - Check or money order enclosed ☐

  - Visa ☐, Master Card ☐, American Express ☐.

Credit Card #: _____ Exp. date _____

Signature: _____

Please send your order form to: Linda Joy Rose, Ph.D.
                                  351 N. Newport Blvd. Suite 528
                                  Newport Beach, CA 92663

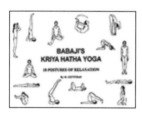